Re-Invention

Brian F Simmons

BRIAN F SIMMONS

ISBN:9798539693336

DEDICATION

I dedicate this work with utmost gratitude to my dear wife Marilyn for the love, companionship and support she has shown during our time together and without whom hardly anything that I have achieved would have come to pass. Also, to my children Maria and Robert and the many friends along the way who have supplied information, encouragement and patience with this novice writer.

This work is further dedicated to Brian Marcus Peck, my brother who I sadly never knew but who was a man of great knowledge, courage, integrity and political acumen.

AUTHOR'S NOTE

I firmly believe that a memoir should be truthful and complete as far as the author is concerned. However, with regard to the other players I may have changed the odd name to protect individual's privacy where appropriate.

With regard to political correctness, please bear in mind that attitudes have changed over time so where I have made comments or quoted something that we would perhaps find unacceptable today that has not been done to give offence but to simply record what was said, thought or done at the time.

To Mollie

With many, many
thanks for your cheerful
patience with this still-
learning photographer.

You may find this of
interest while longing
in the Caribbean sun.

Brian

Contents

RE-INVENTION

INTRODUCTION

A LONG TIME AGO

I grew up in Ashtead, Surrey in the post-war years between 1944 and 1964 during which time I did all the daft childish things and the stupid and occasionally dangerous things one does as a teenager.

My education; whilst good thanks to my parents' generosity in paying for my private school after I failed the eleven-plus, was far from outstanding in terms of the results. So I left school at sixteen with 'O' Levels in just English Language, English Literature and Chemistry.

Apart from school holiday jobs, my first real work was in an electro-chemical research laboratory. It was very interesting but after about eighteen months I tired of the routine and the maths that was starting to assume a greater proportion of my part-time college studies and I ran off to sea as a steward with P&O. Never intended as a career move, it was however a fabulous experience if a very steep learning curve especially in relation to the on-board gay scene of which, as a rather sheltered catholic lad, I was totally ignorant. Sufficient to say, it was educational but definitely not for me. After a short cruise and a five-month round-the-world trip, I left P&O very well-travelled in terms of bars discovered in far-flung places but still unsure about where my life was going.

After a very brief dalliance with the developing supermarket industry (my father's profession), I decided, largely on impulse, to join the Metropolitan Police. This was also quite a shock to the system when it came to finding my way around the seamier side of Lambeth but I loved it despite the fact that keeping in touch with my Surrey friends was a bit difficult. However, when in the summer of '64 my mother was diagnosed with cancer I felt I needed to be closer to home so left the Met and found work selling Rootes Group cars at Ewell in Surrey.

These years eventually became the subject of my first book – Stepping Out from Ashtead.

A FAIR TIME AGO

Being a 1960's motor trader was huge fun in an Arthur Daly sort of way and I really enjoyed the buzz of the deal and the satisfaction derived from turning a profit. I was quite a 'Jack the Lad' around that time but the down side was that a deal too much alcohol was consumed and I found myself on a bit of a downward path which fortunately came to a halt when love came along and I married in 1967. Sadly, my mother was unable to enjoy that time as she had died the previous year.

Marriage, a mortgage and the early arrival of our first child caused me to reluctantly reconsider the motor trade as a lifelong career due to the fluctuations of a commission-based income so in 1968 I rejoined the police service in the Surrey Force. I was certainly not a vocational policeman at that time and freely admit that security of employment, a regular income and the housing allowance comprised a major part of my motivation.

That said I was extremely conscientious and ambitious, seeing advancement through hard work and promotion as the best way to provide for my family's security. Regrettably, my wife could never see things in quite the same long-term way and this, to my mind laudable ambition, eventually proved to be our downfall and after thirteen years we went our separate ways with me being awarded custody of our two children Robert and Maria.

My career in the Surrey force was extremely varied, interesting and successful and I am confident in saying I made a valid contribution in a number of specialist fields even if not as a great 'crime-buster'. However, it takes all sorts.

In 1986 I remarried and had been happily sharing my life with a wonderful lady until after eight years life bowled an unexpected low ball that changed everything overnight. The thirty years to 1994 became the subject of my second memoir 'Until the Lights Went Out'

UP TILL NOW

1994 was a bitter-sweet year. An unforeseen emotional collapse in February pitched me into a terrible place. Without doubt, the consequence of a string of personal crises and insensitive management at work fully described in my last memoir; this crash took me into six months of black depression.

I know we moved house but remember almost nothing about the process of finding our new home or the actual move. Clearly, I must have completed the legal requirements but don't remember that either.

After months of withdrawal, a lot of Prozac and with my wife Marilyn's love and sensitive care I began to surface with the summer only to be greeted in September with the news that the Surrey Constabulary had decided to retire me on the grounds of my ill health. They had been advised that a return to my previous or any similar position was likely to precipitate a further and possibly more serious breakdown.

I said bitter-sweet year because whilst this was absolutely not how I would have wanted to end my police career it did mean I was able to draw a line under the previous six months. It also meant that with the benefit of a monthly pension and useful lump sum we could take our time in deciding how we took our life forward.

In many ways similar to coping with bereavement, it was excruciatingly painful learning to accept that the person I had once been no longer existed.

Reluctantly coming to terms with this reality we decided that without a mortgage or young family to support we could afford to just coast a bit, go with the flow and see what happened.

The following pages are an account of that process, the things we discovered and where the next twenty-five years took us.

PART ONE

WEST SUSSEX

1 FITTLEWORTH

i

Sometimes, even now, I can't believe it actually happened. Unbelievable that we, or certainly I, could ever have been that adventurous. Or perhaps foolhardy would have been a more cynical and accurate assessment of our situation. But anyway, there we were in August 1999, driving down through France to start our new life in Spain.

Our lovely home of five years and much-loved half-acre garden was now someone else's Shangri-La. Our possessions were in store, and our destination was a rented townhouse in the pretty rural village of Santa Maria de Corco in Catalunya about an hour and a half inland from Gerona and Barcelona and in the foothills of the Pyrenees.

However, I'm not in Spain now but living in England having moved four years ago from Peaslake in The Surrey Hills to start the next chapter of our life in West Sussex for the second time. So, what happened?

It would be a huge understatement to say that things didn't exactly pan out as first envisaged but the story really began more than five years earlier.

ooooOoooo

ii

I'd been a police officer in Surrey for almost thirty years, enjoying quite a successful career that had included a variety of duties from uniform patrol through detective duties, police marksman, law and firearms trainer, force recruiting officer, press liaison and IT trainer to career development advisor. After an unusually early promotion to Sergeant, I was doing very well although the marital breakdown and having custody of the children after my divorce undoubtedly held back my progress a bit. Promotion to Inspector eventually came in 1985.

However, towards the end of 1993 for various reasons around management style and internal politics, work was becoming quite hard going and as we had had a very welcome inheritance Marilyn and I were wondering whether I might take early retirement when I reached fifty the following year. This was the earliest age at which it was possible to retire with a pension. Being about two years before my due retirement date it would have meant accepting a small reduction in pension, but on balance we felt it would be worth-while to get out a bit early as we had some ideas we were keen to explore.

A good part of our reasoning was based on the notion, that if possible, one should not put off doing things as one never knows what events are around the corner. We had a bit of a tick list of travel destinations too, so having more or less decided on the early retirement idea we headed off to Thailand in January. I know we enjoyed the trip but curiously I have very little recollection of what I know was a wonderful holiday so perhaps things were already starting to go wrong for me.

Another part of the early exit strategy was to relocate in Sussex as property was cheaper and life a little less hectic just that bit further away from London and outside the Surrey commuter belt. So in pursuit of that goal, whilst I was at work Marilyn set about house hunting in Sussex and we apparently went to see several houses one of which was 'Wingates', the one we eventually bought in Fittleworth but I don't remember any of them.

The crunch came on Valentine's Day 1994 which was a Monday when as I was getting dressed, I suffered a sudden and complete emotional collapse, broke down in tears and was unable to go to work. The doctor signed me off initially for a month with stress and then indefinitely with depression which triggered a referral to the Force psychologist.

While all this was happening, the move went ahead but I have absolutely no memory of it at all although Marilyn tells me I helped out. I must have been on complete automatic pilot.

I know I saw the psychologist a couple of times but again have little recollection of the visits although by about mid-summer the Prozac was beginning to work and I was starting to come round a bit and can remember my joy at the lovely new surroundings I found myself in.

At the time of my break-down, we had been in a rented house having grabbed a cash buyer for our previous place at Horsley in Surrey. This situation gave us the option to have a bit of redecoration done at Wingates before we moved in, so, as I said, by about mid-summer we were in just as my recovery began.

I say recovery but should emphasize it was very tenuous at that point and I was still pretty fragile. The main symptom of this was an almost total inability to stay awake for more than three hours or so or to make even simple decisions such as what I might wear or what to eat. It was very strange given that my whole personality is normally one of secure self-confidence. The other thing that immediately brought on the shakes was any mention of the police and my former job and I certainly couldn't tolerate even driving anywhere near the force HQ in Guildford.

However, in September I had no option but to return there in response to a summons from the Force Medical Officer. I had no idea what to expect and was stunned when he told me the force were proposing to compulsorily retire me. This was apparently because the psychologist had decided that if I returned, a similar or worse breakdown was likely and the force might be seen as lacking in their duty of care.

Well, they say 'it's an ill wind' and while this was far from the way I imagined my career would end I couldn't have been more relieved especially when I studied Police Regulations. I discovered that as I had served more than twenty-six and a half years my pension would be made up to the full amount, neatly dealing with the shortfall we had reckoned on if I retired early of my own volition.

Even after all that it was several years before I could bring myself to go anywhere near the force HQ. Not, I hasten to add, because my time there was so bad but because of the terrible black depression I associated with it in my mind.

All the time I'd been on sick leave I had been receiving sickness benefit and according to the doctors being compulsorily retired did not preclude me from that benefit and so I continued to claim it. However, after another month or two as I began to feel even better the old conscience began to kick in and I wondered at the honesty of continuing to pick up the sickness benefit.

At a pre-retirement course the previous year we had been reminded that as police pensioners we were still of working age in the eyes of the state system. As such, until we found other employment, we were entitled to claim unemployment benefit and so it occurred to me that perhaps I should give up the sickness benefit and proclaim myself ready to work but presently unemployed and so claim the benefit. To this end, I went off to the Job Centre for my interview where I discovered that it was now called 'Jobseekers Allowance' and a condition of which was that one was genuinely seeking work and that to qualify I had to have the jobseekers interview.

The benefits officer sat me down and opened the interview which began with her asking me what I was qualified to do. Well clearly 'police inspector' was out of the question so the next stage was for me to complete a form stating my strengths, skills and so on. *"No problem,"* I thought *"No different to making an internal job application in the force"* and I'd done loads of those over the years.

As I started to write out my management skills; leadership, ideas man, problem-solving, planning, team-building, budgetary control, time management, etc. I started to tremble. I felt as though someone had just literally kicked my feet from under me and I looked up through tear-filled eyes at the benefits officer.

She smiled gently and said, *"You're not ready yet Brian. I just wish everyone were as honest as you. Give yourself a bit more time and don't be in too much of a hurry. Don't forget you've paid in for years so just relax and accept the sick pay. I think you still need it"*

I never did go back because it slowly dawned on me that I was no longer the same person; no longer the team leader and problem solver but a different person. The most difficult thing was learning to accept over time that the other person really had gone and that I was now someone else. Not unlike a bereavement when the recovery process lies in getting used to the idea that a person has gone and that you have to move on, except that in this case, the person who had gone was the old me.

iii

Wingates was a pretty three bedroom detached house in about half an acre of garden and located in a rural lane in the village of Fittleworth to the west of Pulborough. It had been extended to provide a modern kitchen and a lovely long garden room and so had plenty of ground floor accommodation even if it was a bit short in the bedroom department. Still, there were only the two of us so it was perfect really. The lane was a no-through-road of barely a dozen houses ending in the woods of the Stopham estate and so was ideal for walking our dog, Benjy.

The main garden to the rear backed onto woodland where we could also walk. It had been landscaped to a degree with many interesting trees and shrubs, a real well and a raised circular terrace ideal for sitting out.

The house was sited a bit lower than the lane so there was a slight problem that the survey identified with surface water when it rained. This drained off the road surface and ran towards the house where it ponded along the front wall and ran through the air bricks so not exactly an ideal situation. It did however provide a good supply of water to a Victoria plum that had been trained against the south-facing wall and was incredibly prolific as a result.

There was also an issue of parking space because the drive was long and narrow which meant that we were often shuffling cars around when either one of us wanted to go out. The single garage presumably dated from the 1930's when the house was built and was nowhere near large enough for even one modern car nor the storage we seem to need these days so we decided that a new garage and drive were needed. Apart from deciding in principle what we'd do, we then agreed that autumn and winter weren't the ideal time to start such a project so it went on the back burner while we sorted out other aspects of our new life.

iv

One such aspect was the business Marilyn had started a couple of years previously. This was a mobile clothes retail business selling to residents of sheltered housing schemes for whom a trip to browse around high street shops was difficult or impossible. By virtue of her previous involvement with the management of such schemes with a local authority in Surrey, Marilyn knew of the potential market but also had a personal connection with some of the wardens whose agreement was needed to go in and hold sales.

The idea really took off and in no time she had extended the client base to locations in south London and Sussex. It was very labour intensive though and most evenings following a sale were spent re-folding and bagging the stock for the dear old ladies to treat it like a jumble sale again tomorrow. Also, we didn't have the funds to hold a vast stock so most weekends would see us driving up to Commercial Road in the East End and traipsing around the wholesalers to buy up clothes.

The other difficult aspect was that Marilyn was running the whole operation out of the back of our estate car which meant packing up all the stock and dismantling the rails after each sale. This was doing her back no good at all so I suggested we get a van. A second-hand Renault Trafic hi-top duly arrived and I had a ramp made up so she could simply run the rails up into the van, rope them in position and head off home or wherever. By this time, I was also partly involved in helping Marilyn out from time to time but by no means full-time which left me feeling a bit spare so I started to look for something to do on a casual basis and here my old love and interest in cars resurfaced.

I like nice cars and with Harwoods of Pulborough on the doorstep selling Rolls-Royce, Bentley, Jaguar and Landrover it seemed the ideal place to see if they had anything I could do. The 'trained police driver' label undoubtedly helped because they took me on immediately as a casual which meant they could say when they wanted me and I likewise could decide daily if I wanted to do a few hours. As a job, it was nothing fancy but that didn't matter as I'd had enough of the management and career thing.

This was simple and mainly geared around early collections of cars for service with a break in the middle of the day before returning them in the evening. Mainly it was fairly local driving with the occasional longer job. I seemed to get most of the longer ones as I'd expressed that preference and a regular trip was to take a Jaguar loan car to Edgware Road in London and bring back a magnificent bright red Bentley Continental.

I must say, there is little to compare with the way the traffic seems to part in front of you when driving such a vehicle, apart perhaps a high speed 'blue light run' in a police car when the traffic opens up even more quickly. One day I had to take a train down to Christchurch in Dorset and bring back an Aston Martin convertible. That was a pretty awesome drive and very difficult to resist the temptation to see what it could do along the A303. Before you ask, I'm not saying.

Marilyn's clothing business was by no means full time so when I started working for Harwoods she also started looking for something else to do and responded to an advert for a 'lunch cover assistant' at the local Tourist Information Office in Midhurst. She enjoyed this as it ticked a lot of her 'job satisfaction' boxes and although we didn't know, it would lead on to much more in the whole tourism sector.

During the previous three years, my son Rob had been up at university and in July we had his graduation to attend. He was the first of my family to be awarded a degree and I must say it was with a huge sense of pride that we watched him in his mortarboard and gown stepping up to receive his degree certificate.

Before meeting Marilyn, I had been pretty lukewarm about foreign travel, perhaps thinking *"Been there, done that"* simply on the strength of my travels when working with P&O in my late teens. I'd certainly visited many places but to be frank I was in a lot of bars around the world but had very little experience of the countries themselves that would qualify me as a 'traveller'. I guess I was rather inclined to the view that I could discover all I needed to know from books or TV which horrified Marilyn as she had been an experienced independent traveller since her late teens. *"You can read about it but you can't experience places without going and immersing yourself,"* she said, and ever since then, we have done a lot of immersion travelling.

These trips had included India, Tunisia and Egypt, and then Thailand as well as a couple of trips to Spain. Maybe it was the Moorish elements of our trip to Andalucía that spiked our interest because in January we were off again. This time it was to Morocco and the ancient city of Marrakech.

Morocco and Marrakech were amazing; dirty, beautiful, interesting, and fascinating in equal measure, and if a travel 'experience' was what we were after we had it in spades on that trip. The main Jemaa el-Fnaa square in Marrakech is a scene to behold at any time of day or night with something different to interest or catch the eye.

Colourfully dressed water sellers were not above chasing you across the square if they spotted you snatching a long-range snap without offering a few Dirhams for the privilege. Meanwhile, the Henna artists vied with jugglers, snake charmers, and acrobats for your attention and the storytellers and scribes just carried on their daily business which was certainly not solely for the tourists as they were always surrounded by crowds of locals in rapt attention. At night the whole scene changed when the dozens of illuminated food stalls arrived offering a vast range of freshly cooked hot and delicious street food.

We explored the rather dark and frightening depths of the medina with the various 'souks' specializing in many different trades from carpet weaving to silver-smithing. Several cultural museums were on our list but one highlight was the beautiful Majorelle Garden (also known as the Yves St Laurent Gardens) with its formal layout of paths, water, and exotic plants along with the vibrant colours; in particular, the vivid cobalt blue and yellows that decorate many of the building.

Another day we drove through the beautiful Ourika Valley into the mountains to visit Berber villages strung out along the river that had claimed so many lives over the years with sudden flash floods following mountain storms.

In a market along the way, we saw a dentist's 'surgery' that amounted to no more than a chair out in the open where you could get a tooth pulled and then choose a set of dentures from a jumbled pile of second-hand ones on a table.

Back in 1989 when living in Guildford we had taken a thirteen-year-old Spanish student called Alex as a house guest in the summer holidays. As a result, we got to know his family and began a relationship with Spain and things Spanish that was to become a major feature of our lives. The main issue at that time for me was frustration with the inability to speak the language and communicate with the lovely family in Barcelona that had taken us so warmly to their hearts. So in October of 1994, I went on a language course in Andalucía and afterwards Marilyn came out and we enjoyed a week together exploring Granada and the surrounding area.

The course was a great experience and worth a word or two as its influence on our lives, although we didn't know it then, was set to be dramatic. The venue was the tiny village of Ferreirola, one of 'Los Pueblos Blancos' or white villages beautifully situated at 1,000 m on the southern slope of the Sierra Nevada National Park. The mild climate of the valley, the many mountain springs, and the rich vegetation make up the scenery around this former Moorish village. The village is situated away from the main tourist routes and the tranquillity is total.

The bed and breakfast business operated there called Sierra y Mar takes the name from its location about midway between the high sierra and the sea and because it is possible on the same day to ski the mountains and water ski at the coast. Happily, its blue door still welcomes guests although now a good bit upgraded compared to the somewhat basic but charming accommodation back then. We were about eight students in number including a German girl and two Scandinavian doctors and their wives. The whole group was divided into two roughly according to our language ability and the classes were taught by a couple of locals who I believe were currently unemployed or former teachers. (www.sierraymar.com)

It was quite delightful as breakfast was taken al-fresco under a mulberry tree in the patio garden and then we went off onto the roof terraces for four hours of class each day. Beyond that, the arrangements were very relaxed. Sepp and Inge the hosts offered guided walks in the surrounding hills or we were free to go off and practice our language with the locals.

The village was very small with no amenities apart from one bar where we and the locals gathered most evenings. On the outskirts of the village, there was a small Flamenco school and the students also came to the bar where sometimes we were treated to an entirely impromptu entertainment. One of the students might start by simply tapping out a rhythm on the table to be joined by one or two of the others and that might go on for a while before one of them would begin with the flamenco singing. No one ever danced. It was just rhythm and song. Simple, basic, and quite beautiful for its simplicity.

I had booked to be there for two weeks but after one week all the other students left apart from the German girl and she made it very clear that as it was to be just the two of us, we could perhaps be practising something more interesting and personal than a few words of Spanish if you get my meaning. Well, another time, in another life, or had I been young free, and single I could well have been up for whatever she had in mind but I lost my nerve and decided to leave too.

I set off alone to meander slowly through the beautiful foothills and villages of the area refining my newly acquired but rather basic Spanish while heading for Granada where I was to meet Marilyn the next weekend. We had a wonderful few days in the historic and atmospheric city exploring the back streets, the fabulous Generalife gardens and even treated ourselves to a ridiculously expensive night in the Alhambra Parador hotel which was within the palace itself.

Reflecting later on the village B and B experience I remember thinking *"Perhaps we could do that."* Little did I know.

v

The summer of '94 was great because more or less as I started to emerge from the depression that had overwhelmed me, we celebrated my 50th birthday with a really great party. We hired a marquee and booked Hedley Kay a singer we knew from Surrey to entertain us. I knew Hedley from a folk club in Leatherhead back in the '70s and first had him to sing for us at my 40th birthday party in Guildford. Irish by birth his soft accent brings a lovely quality to many of the standard pop and folk songs as well as his own compositions. A lovely nostalgic if slightly noisy evening to get the neighbours chattering.

By the end of the year, I guess we had settled in after a fashion although I am not entirely sure what the locals thought of these new arrivals especially as we kept disappearing to foreign parts or I would periodically turn up on the drive in a posh Bentley.

Or, when not driving smart cars, we would head off in the Renault Trafic like Mr and Mrs White-Van-Man and then return lugging bags of clothes to be stashed in the garage. I would love to have been a proverbial 'fly on the wall' around a few local dinner tables to hear what they were making of us.

For our part, we loved everything about it. True to say, there was not a lot to Fittleworth itself as the only real amenity apart from the pub was the village store and Post Office. Unfortunately, this was run by a man and his elderly mother, both of whom must have been at the end of the queue when a sense of humour was being dished out. I think in the whole time we were there I never saw either of them smile so it did not come as a great surprise to see when passing through Fittleworth a couple of years ago that the shop was then selling antiques. Since actually returning to live nearby we have been delighted to find that there is now an excellent community shop run by volunteers and it even includes a coffee shop and children's play area.

Apart from the Co-Op in Petworth, there were no supermarkets nearby (although there are now two in Pulborough) so for a big shop, we had to head for Horsham or Chichester which were about sixteen miles each.

Near to Chichester of course we had Goodwood, the motor circuit where I had spent so much time back in the 60s and which, by the time I am talking about was still moth-balled following its closure to public events in 1966.

However, there was the Goodwood Hotel and Health Club which, as we were fairly well-off at the time we joined and used to enjoy their swimming and gym facilities regularly.

We particularly liked the nearby woods of the Stopham estate at the end of our road where we could walk our little dog Benjy directly from the house. The woods, that were all part of the Stopham estate were mostly chestnut interspersed with mature oak. They were well managed too and it was interesting to observe how in successive years sections were maintained by coppicing, the cuttings being destined to become walking sticks. The bizarre element however, as I discovered by chatting to the contractor, was that the sticks were sold to a firm in Germany who made the sticks which were then sold back to the NHS. Apparently, the skills and equipment to do the work were no longer available in England. I thought that very sad.

vi

With the spring of '95, we turned our attention back to the garage and parking issue. We both fancied one of the rustic style cart-shed sort of garages that we thought would work perfectly in our rural lane and sent off for a brochure to one of the many firms supplying them. Well, apart from almost falling over at the prices quoted, I loved how the brochure showed an excellent detailed drawing of the timber construction. I'd always been a bit keen on woodworking and said to Marilyn *"It's certainly large but it's very basic carpentry. I reckon I could build it."* How could we have possibly known how those few words were going to impact the next twenty years?

Having more or less decided that's what I'd do I set about a rough design, sufficient to know what footprint was needed, and then we went in search of someone to help solve the driveway and water problems. A local guy by the name of Jim Allfrey specialized in drives and groundworks so he was contracted to dig out almost all the sloping front garden, lay a spacious forecourt, and put down an eight by five-metre concrete slab for me to use as a garage base in due course.

Ideally, I would have liked to build the classic oak-framed three-bay barn which would have been very costly. However, as we are not going to be around in three hundred years to see it, I decided that only the front frame needed to be in oak, and the rest could be in softwood. As it happened, I had a ready supply of salvaged timber from the house we had demolished in the course of our Horsley rebuild project a couple of years before.

We had managed to agree with the new owners that we could leave the timber there along with my tractor (just another one of those little projects you get involved in) until we were settled in our new home.

So, with the help of long-time friend Clive and a rented lorry we brought the timber to Fittleworth. It was not going to be anywhere near enough to do the whole job but would certainly save us a few hundred pounds. I also hired a haulier to collect the tractor from Horsley so bringing to a close our connection with that area.

Lulu the grey Fergy tractor I restored over several years at Horsley.

2   WOOD BECOMES MY FRIEND

i

It's one thing to say I'd done a bit of woodworking over the years but the truth was that making a little oak table at an evening class plus the usual domestic bit of DIY shelf or MDF cupboard construction was actually about the extent of my experience. I had also done a satisfactory set of plans for a very basic small extension on our former police house at Merrow a few years before. A tad different to a forty square metre garage but *"Hey-ho - it may be big but it's hardly rocket science"* or so went my internal pep talk as I realized what I'd set myself up for.

The first thing was to check out the local authority planning rules to see if we could do it at all which happily proved to be no problem. But what I hadn't thought of was that such a construction, even if non-habitable was going to have to comply with Building Regulations and that detailed drawings would be required for both planning permission and to satisfy Building Control. Working out material quantities was quite a big part of the job and I soon discovered that a trade account at the local builders' merchant was going to be useful and save me some money too and so B.S.Services was born.

It's possible that at the time I was still to some extent in recovery mode and that while I had the vision about the garage project, I was still rather lacking in energy to get it off the starting blocks. So much so in fact that we decided in June '95 to turn our backs on it for a bit longer and set off for a couple of weeks to drive down through France to Spain and spend a bit more time with Alex's family in Barcelona and the surrounding area which, it must be admitted, was becoming a bit of a magnet for us.

Previous visits had been by air but on this occasion, we decided to drive as I had recently bought a new Nissan sports car and was itching to get it out onto the open continental roads. So, with dog Benjy and our new house in the capable care of dear elderly friends Fred and Edie we set off south.

This was the first time I had driven through France and while the temptation to hit the motorways and cover the ground in the new car was very strong, we soon found that frequent diversions onto local roads were definitely worthwhile. Here we discovered pretty almost traffic-free roads, meandering rivers, delightful towns, and villages with their very reasonably priced Chambre-d'hôte accommodation. We delighted in the farmers' markets with their wonderful selection of fruit and vegetables where we picked up our cheese, tomatoes, fruit, and wine for leisurely riverside picnics along the way. It truly was quite idyllic.

Me relaxing beside the Vezere river in Montignac in France

Arriving in Catalunya we were kindly hosted by Alex's family at their weekend house which turned out to be quite an impressive four-bedroom property along the coast a few miles north of Barcelona. From here we continued to explore the surrounding area little realizing the extent to which it was getting under our skin. Anyway, after an enjoyable three weeks, we headed for home.

The trip must have renewed our energy and strengthened resolve because we came back fired with enthusiasm to make a start on transforming Wingates to our needs, the first stage of which was to be the new garage workshop.

It was one thing ordering prepared timber from the local builders' merchant but the oak was different again. I found a local forestry and sawmill company where I went to order the eight-inch square posts and beams I was planning to use for the main front frame of the barn. I intended to include the curved crucks or corner braces and was fully expecting to have to do all the mortice and tenon cutting myself, so was delighted to see that the yard was able to provide joints pre-cut using the large machines at their disposal. At £10 per joint, I said *"Yes please."* And so, a few days later the four vertical posts, three cross beams, and six curved braces arrived on site.

My son Rob witnessed the first post going up.

On 1ˢᵗ July 1995, the first post was erected, and in the process I discovered how very heavy green oak is and was immediately faced with the problem of getting the cross beams up onto the vertical posts. However, a few days later the problem was solved thanks to Marilyn's nephew Geoff and his weight-lifting gym partner. On the day I planned to raise the front frame they turned up and with relative ease between the four of us and a moment when a beam was supported on Marilyn's head, we managed to get the cross beams mounted on the tenoned posts. We eased in the corner crucks and suddenly there it was; a complete front frame and immediately it was possible to see how the whole thing would look. I was thrilled and so grateful for their help.

I was very much feeling my way with the building process but quite quickly my confidence grew and before long I was hopping up and down ladders, and running along beams as first the stud walls, the oak cladding, and then the roof took shape. I was very grateful to Marilyn's father Tom who, whilst then an antique restorer, had learned his basic woodworking skills in the army years before and so was able to offer advice where needed.

Marilyn's father Tom, offering his carpentry advice.

Whilst I was able to do the carpentry described I had no idea whatever about roof tiling so a local contractor was brought in and in no time at all, it seemed the felt and battens gave us the weatherproof structure, and then some nice mellow second-hand tiles completed the job. I had decided that two of the bays would be left open for the cars but that the third would be closed with an attractive pair of oak doors I also made and then fitted out as my new workshop.

I think the neighbours were initially a little sceptical at this rank amateur embarking on such a sizeable project but as it progressed the passing glances became more and more admiring. One day a builder who was working in the lane stopped by for a chat. Admiring the roof, he asked where I'd learnt my carpentry and was amazed when I told him I never had apart from the experience he had watched over the recent months. I explained that every rafter length was calculated with my old school trigonometry tables and he laughed as he explained the time I could have saved by making up a pattern rafter from which to cut the others.

Garage complete with my Nissan also in view

However, he was very complimentary and explained that with the chippies who he employed he regarded it as acceptable work if *"it fitted where it touched"* I wasn't totally sure what he meant but got the gist of it.

I'd certainly taken my time on the garage building to the point when

Marilyn was getting a bit peeved with the place looking like a building site. She's a great one for tidying things up so eventually under a bit of pressure from management by the spring of '96 I had the doors completed on the third bay. I then got the place fitted out as a very respectable workshop with everything in its place and looking ship-shape although, to be honest at that point I didn't have much idea what I might be doing in there.

The next thing that happened was a complete and pleasant surprise.

During the year I'd been working on the garage new neighbours had arrived next door and one day the husband came round and asked if I could build him a garage the same as ours. Well, the proverbial feather could have knocked me over but I immediately saw the opportunity and said I'd need to think about how I costed it before I could give him a price. Building my own, I had not worked every day and certainly not thought about counting the hours or days spent so I had to try to assess what would be a reasonable price to suggest. Material costs were not a problem as I had all the recent records for that but how to cost my time was the great unknown so I took a different approach.

I was going to be working as a one-man band and I thought that working proper eight-hour days I should be able to do it in a couple of months subject to weather so I asked myself the question *"How much would I want for two months full time hard physical work?" Would I do it for a thousand? Thinking back on it – definitely not. But how about five grand?"*

Now remember that this was 1996 and £2500 for a month's work was about £125 a day which back then was more than I'd earned in the police.

I certainly didn't have much of a business head on at that time because I took my pension into account and not wanting to overstate my quote decided that I could live with that price for my time. Then by taking into account the price my ground-worker and roofer had charged and the material costs I came up with the figure of £16000.

Frankly, to me at that time the idea of anyone spending that sort of money on a garage was a flight of fancy but anyway I went for it and the quote was accepted without a second thought and I knew I'd underpriced it. Never mind, "*We live and learn.*" I did laugh though when he told me that in order to pay for it he might have to sell a couple of the parrots he'd bred. I couldn't really believe that anyone could pay thousands for a bird that might just die and then I couldn't stop thinking about John Cleese and the dead parrot sketch.

In the event I completed the build in a little under six weeks so had pretty much come up smelling of roses and feeling rather smug about the whole thing. Then as if that wasn't success enough, I received enquiries from other people for smaller woodworking jobs like building gates and shelves and small items of furniture.

I didn't have much in the way of power tools at the time and as I was self-taught, I knew I was probably missing a lot of tricks due to lack of training so I signed up for an Introduction to Woodworking course at West Dean College which was not far from us at Singleton.

It was a great course and I came home with a lot of tricks and techniques learnt and a shopping list of further tools and machinery that I would need if I was going to continue to develop this activity which I was feeling very positive about.

Almost the first machine I decided I needed was a decent saw bench and I found a good second-hand radial arm saw which I bought and set up across the back of the remaining two garage bays so limiting at a stroke its use as a car garage at all. I wished I'd had the vision to build it two metres deeper but I hadn't and that was that.

However, my purchase of the new saw was almost immediately justified when orders for not one but two more oak garages came in. "*Wow! This is really starting to look promising.*" I thought especially as Jim Allfrey and Tom Weston the roofer had suggested that they could wait for their payment until each build was finished so easing my cash flow situation.

During the years '96 to '98 jobs continued to come in and it became clear that I had established quite a nice little business as a woodworking handyman and had by that time more or less stopped driving for Harwoods apart from the very occasional job to help them out.

ii

Whilst all the new and interesting woodworking stuff was going on Marilyn was still running the mobile clothing van as well as working part-time at the Tourist Office so was almost a bit busier than she wanted to be. Also, she was having some doubts about continuing with the clothes van. It was certainly a very good commercial formula and the margins were very worthwhile owing to the low overheads but the repetitive aspect of it was very boring and she started to feel it was time to move on. Happily, this coincided with a woman expressing an interest in taking the business over. To be honest we both thought she hadn't appreciated the amount of work involved and was just attracted by the idea of owning a business.

However, after apparently taking on board all our warnings about the work, she bought the business which amounted to a van full of stock and a diary of future booking and we walked away. By way of celebration, we went off on a Concorde Champagne flight which was fabulous and so great to have done it together especially given what happened to Concorde since then. Actually, it was my second flight as Marilyn had bought me a similar experience for my fortieth birthday in 1984. She has always had such brilliant and original birthday ideas.

A few weeks later our reservations were confirmed when we heard that the clothing business had indeed folded which was particularly sad given the amount of work Marilyn had put in and also for the disappointment we knew would be felt by our loyal and rather dependent customers.

Having freed ourselves of the clothing business and after a brief spell taking stock, we began to cast around in our minds for other opportunities, not so much for their earning potential but as an activity to add further interest to life. But of course, if anything should happen to offer additional income opportunity, so much the better.

There was the germ of an idea lurking that had its origins back in the police years. Canteen conversation used, among other things like cars and women, often to include reflections about what one might do on retirement from the job. For me and most of my colleagues, this meant around the age of 50 – 55 or thereabouts, because for lower and intermediate ranks the period of service was thirty years to full pension entitlement.

One thing that used to come up was the notion of getting rid of the mortgage by taking the money and heading off to the west country where the same amount bought more than in Surrey (at least it did back then). Having relocated, quite a few, including me, fancied the idea of starting a B&B.

Marilyn and I chewed the idea over a bit and decided to investigate the possibility of actually doing it where we were in Fittleworth. There was certainly no bed space in the house but we had the single garage that we thought would easily provide a decent bedroom and the adjoining tool shed could be converted to provide a very nice bathroom. It would mean a good bit of work including raising the roof height to be continuous with the existing garage but we were up for that.

A few years previously we had stayed at a B and B near Chichester where much the same arrangement applied. Nice bedrooms were provided in a former garage while a guests' sitting and breakfast rooms were in the main house. We got on very well with our neighbours Mike and Jill and as the conversion we had in mind was going to need planning permission we went around to bounce the idea off them. To our surprise and disappointment, they said in the nicest possible way that as our planned work would impact their existing view, they would feel obliged to oppose it.

In hindsight, we probably rolled over too easily but they were in all other ways lovely neighbours, and not wanting to upset them we ditched that project although not the idea. What that left us with was the need to find another home with suitable existing accommodation or decide to abandon the whole plan.

It might seem that we were hasty given the virtually idyllic work-life balance I have described. Whilst it was in many ways pretty well perfect and we had done so much to the property, it was, at the end of the day just a box. We both believe that a home is what the occupants make it rather than the building itself and as for the handyman business I had developed; well, that could be moved and re-established in another location. As we were by then quite fired up with the idea, we set about looking for suitable properties. We had details of many and went to look at quite a few but only two of which were serious contenders.

One was, by strange coincidence, very near Storrington where we now live, and was already operating as a bed and breakfast business. It was a single storey building beautifully adapted to provide four en suite bedrooms along with the necessary breakfast space and guest sitting room. It was alongside the main road but set well back and nicely secluded with plenty of parking space. In many ways perfect.

Someone must have been watching our backs that day because after viewing the property Marilyn said *"Let's go and have a chat with the neighbours."*

We had never done such a thing before but thank goodness we did because we then really got the whole story. There was an issue between them and the property we were looking at about the shared driveway and the council's refusal to allow another entrance to be created onto the main road. But more significant was a dispute over the neighbour's plan to create a campsite with holiday chalets in their field right behind and adjoining what would have been our garden. We left never to return.

We often pass the place which is no longer trading as a B&B and as far as can be seen from the road, the chalets have not appeared. Life is full of *'what might have beens'* isn't it but of course any of the things that might have been fantastic could equally have been disastrous. So hardly even any point in wondering. Just move on. I would need to remember that in the future.

The other property was also perfectly arranged and located much closer to the coast at Birdham. Also situated beside the road and whilst set back it was much more open with a wide private entrance and loads of parking space. It was a former care home with more than enough bedrooms for our purposes and like the last was in many ways perfect as a B&B to pick up passing trade close to Chichester Marina and the popular beach at The Witterings.

We actually agreed to buy this one and whilst the necessary admin was going through (and fortunately before exchange) we took a friend down to have a look one Sunday evening. Waiting to pull out on the road we were both suddenly aware of the loud and frequent *whoosh, whoosh, whoosh* of the passing traffic and immediately knew there was no way we could cope with that. Thanks once again guardian angel or whoever. We withdrew our offer and as at that time there was nothing else remotely suitable, we called a halt for the time being.

iii

Apart from the brief period described above, the beauty about this time for us was that whilst we were keeping fairly busy, we were working to our timetable rather than someone else's and could pretty much do what we wanted and whenever it suited us. Compared to our previous quite highly stressed professional lives this was a very welcome arrangement.

With this flexibility came the freedom to travel and around this time we went off on further trips to Spain where we became progressively closer to Alex's family in Barcelona and more entranced by the rural areas of Catalunya. One aspect of the area that we especially liked was the landscape and rural architecture and in particular the big old farmhouses in honeyed stone that seemed to blend so beautifully into the earthy tones of the landscape. They are called masias which is the Catalan word for a farmhouse but we were rather saddened by the number that seemed to be falling down.

There were two factors operating here. One was rural depopulation owing to the shortage of work which in turn was due partly to the increasing mechanisation of farming and also the disinclination of younger people to follow their parents' occupations.

However, where farms were apparently still being worked, we noticed that owners appeared relaxed about allowing the old family home to fall down whilst building new and modern nearby. Well as we Brits are generally quite romantic not to say soppy about old atmospheric houses and trying to bring them back to life it wasn't too long before we started to imagine what it might be like to take on such a project. Although undefined it was probably around then that the germ of an idea came into being that would have far-reaching effects.

iv

Shortly after Marilyn wound up the clothing business we had her father down to visit us, who as I mentioned was an antique restorer and cabinet maker. In the course of conversation, he mentioned some cane seat chairs he had to work on and how he was finding it very hard to find someone to do the cane weaving. This piqued Marilyn's interest and as much for interest sake as anything else she decided that she would learn how to do it herself and found a course at a local adult education centre. Whilst on the course she also joined the Basket-makers Association which includes the related skill of chair-caning.

Having completed the course I think she did a couple of pieces for her father who mentioned it to an antique dealer in Dorking and the next we knew was that she had the makings of a little craft business going as the dealer got in touch and started bringing items down for her to repair.

Somehow the word spread and it wasn't long before we had everything from single chairs to five-foot-long benches and even a French bed where the foot panel had apparently been kicked through. I must say it did amuse us to think of the bedroom antics that might have wrought such damage.

It was actually easier for Marilyn to completely re-cane a piece than repair it although it was a good bit more expensive. I remember on one occasion when a dealer had insisted on repair that we had this bed-head laid out on the floor as we gingerly tried to insert short lengths of new cane to patch up holes and secure each one with super glue. In the event, I think total replacement would have been the cheaper and longer-lasting option but we did what the customer wanted and took the money thank you.

One day a dealer turned up with something for Marilyn and seeing my workshop said *"What do you do?"* I said *"Oh just bits and pieces of woodworking."* So she asked, *"Would you like to do some bits and pieces for me too?"*

And so was born another little period of my life. Jenny and her partner Mike were antique dealers from Warnham with a shop in Petworth which is a well-known local antique centre. Their business was based on buying in France at fairs and bringing stock back to sell-on, either in the shop or the trade.

Neither of them were woodworkers and although Jenny knew a bit about finishing and polishing, they needed someone to do the necessary repairs. The other thing that was difficult for them was that in the bustle of a trade fair they needed to make decisions quickly based on sometimes limited inspection so that on occasions, once I started to look an item over it would turn out to need more work and therefore more cost than they might have budgeted for.

However, this became the next and for us, a quite lucrative phase and I was working somewhere between half and full time for Jenny and Mike. Initially, most of the work was done at their home but it soon outgrew that arrangement and they took on a warehouse to store and repair the stock.

I forgot to mention that when the woodworking started to get going and seeing the potential to develop this little business, I had placed an advert in the parish magazine. This produced quite a bit of work too and although we were still able to suit ourselves regarding the level at which we worked the inclination, of course, was to always take jobs on if possible. So it would be true to say we were neither under nor over-occupied but most importantly it was very much on our terms.

3 WE DIVERSIFY

i

Now most people might think that this set up would have been enough but with Marilyn around, believe me, life was (and still is) never dull.

I tended to, and still do, pick up most of the news I need from the main TV bulletins or newspaper headlines, but not my dear wife. No, she reads in far more depth and as a result is invariably better informed, certainly about local news, than I am; so one day from behind the paper I heard *"How do you fancy looking after a Roman villa?*

I said *"What's this a new holiday idea?*
"No. It's at Bignor. They are looking for a couple of people to look after the Roman Villa there to give the full-time wardens some time off. What do you think?"

I must say I was intrigued so Marilyn found out a bit more and it turned out that the wardens were a couple who lived beside the place and were pretty much fully occupied during the season with very little time off. What was needed were a couple, or at least two people who could do a couple of days a week or an occasional long weekend to let the other two get away.

Anyway, long story short, we applied and got the job. It wasn't loads of money but was certainly something a bit different. The site is just north of the South Downs and a short way off the main A29 which was the old Stane Street of the Romano-British period around 100-400 AD and ran from London to Chichester.

First discovered in 1811, the site came to light when a farmer's plough struck a large stone. The site was excavated and the remains of a large villa unearthed that included some of the most impressive Roman mosaic floors in the country. The site was probably occupied by high-status farmers that were either Roman immigrants or Roman-British as a result of intermarriage or similar cultural integrations. When the Romans eventually cluttered off back south to the sun around 410AD British culture deteriorated and places like the Bignor villa were abandoned, robbed for building materials and simply overgrown and buried by time.

Not blind to the commercial potential of such an interesting find the landowner opened the site as a tourist attraction and further excavations in 1815 discovered the full extent of the site which extended over several acres.

The Bignor villa has always remained in private ownership but has been well conserved. It is quite common practice following excavations for archaeological remains to be fully documented and then re-buried for protection but in this case, the owners decided to build flint and thatched buildings to preserve the site and probably more importantly its commercial potential as a visitor attraction. Curiously, the cover building themselves are now also listed for protection.

Our job at the villa was to manage the visitors. That meant selling them tickets and souvenirs which Marilyn did from a little glass office at the entrance and to feed and water them which I did.

There never had been electricity laid on to the site, which is probably one reason why it was only open from March to October when the days are long and light enough.

However, this did mean that my tea and coffee production relied on a gas urn to boil the water. Anyway, that was no problem and I enjoyed serving the drinks, biscuits and sweets and chatting to the visitors. Our little dog Benjy was a bit of a star turn too as he was very cute and always managed to attract a lot of attention and fussing.

A view of a Roman Hypocaust under a mosaic floor.

Some days when we were on duty there were pre-booked guided tours that Gerry the full-time warden had to come over and do but after a while following him around, I learnt the script myself and then I also did the tours.

Once I knew the information, I enjoyed it and it was very similar to the days when I was in the police public relations office and had to take groups of visitors around the HQ complex. There's nothing like having a bunch of people hanging on your every word and laughing at your jokes (which certainly didn't happen at home – she'd heard them all of course) and so it was quite a little ego trip.

This was the café/shop where I served the refreshments.

So at this point, I had my occupational pension; we were travelling whenever we could but in addition, I was running what by then had become quite a busy little woodworking handyman business. By that time I had completed two more of what we started to call 'Brian's Barns' so my handiwork was around the village for all to see as well as in the parish mag. For her part, Marilyn was still working for the Tourist Information Office in Midhurst and then later in the Petworth office as well as repairing the odd bit of caned furniture.

ii

As if the Roman Villa job wasn't enough, on another well-remembered day when she was again behind the local paper the voice said this time *"There's a job here with your name on it."* I thought *"Pity you can't find one with* **your** *name on it."* but what I said was *"Oh really. What's that then?"*

She started to read *"A guy at Goodwood Motor Circuit is looking for skid-pan instructors and needs someone with an advanced driving background and training experience. That's you isn't it?"* I have to admit I was immediately intrigued as I was interested in anything to do with cars and motor racing so I picked up the phone and arranged to meet Colin Wells.

Colin had a lease on the skid-pan at the Goodwood circuit where he ran a business called Skid Control and as the name suggests was about driver training on the subject of both avoiding and recovering from skids when driving. He had been operating a while and was finding it difficult to cover all the courses himself so he wanted to set up a small pool of instructors who could assist him.

Actually, my driving background wasn't what in the police we would have called very advanced. I had done what was known as the Standard Car Course which qualified us to drive normal patrol cars and I also came out with a grade as '*suitable for traffic dept*' which would have required more intensive training still. However, the standard course was at a level significantly above the Ministry of Transport driving test requirement as it was at that time. I had also been a trainer in the police so had the required instructional skills and got the job.

I was probably only required to work three or four times a month so it wasn't a big deal but I certainly enjoyed it. The first thing of course was for Colin to teach me how to induce, avoid and control skidding. The beauty of the skid pan was that it was possible to get into a monumental skid at about five or six miles per hour so there was no danger involved as the worst you could do was to slide into the tyre wall or the bank so no great harm done.

The cars were old Ford Sierras with virtually bald and over-inflated tyres while the very smooth tarmac surface was treated with a 'slick' compound and then sprayed with water. Never mind driving, it was not even that easy to stand up on it.

There were two main client groups, one of which I liked very much and the other much less so. The groups I disliked were the corporate crowd. The Goodwood Circuit used to offer these corporate days when groups of, almost invariably male 'yuppies' would turn up and be given a variety of motoring and sometimes flying experiences.

Depending on the package that had been agreed this usually included being driven around the circuit in one or more very quick cars before perhaps being allowed to drive a lap or two themselves. Then might come a '4x4 experience' and then I think there was some sort of 'dune buggy' course they were let loose on. Some of the packages even included the chance to drive a single-seater racing car plus helicopter or fixed-wing 'trial lessons'. So, by the time they got to the skid pan which seemed invariably to be the last element, they were well fired-up and all they really wanted to do was see how dramatically they could spin the cars and any question of 'skid control' was about the last thing on their minds. Our role in all of this was to keep something of a handle on events, a smile on our faces, stop them wrecking the cars but still send them away happy. For me, it was a slightly difficult circle to square especially with my natural instructional instincts operating.

On the other hand altogether, the clients I loved were those people who seriously wanted to understand how and why cars skid and how to avoid such potentially lethal situations when it happens at normal road speeds. Within this group again were those thoughtful and caring parents who brought their offspring along soon after passing the basic driving test. This was always in my view, the best possible time to try to instill some awareness and knowledge about what actually causes a car to skid and how to react when it does.

Very few people had ever given any thought to the fact that when driving, your life is dependent on four hand-sized areas of rubber in contact with the road and that anything that interferes with the friction between those two surfaces can easily kill you. That 'anything' might be water, black ice, wet leaves, loose gravel or even excessive speed. When spelt out it is a very salutary experience and when demonstrated how at even five miles an hour a car can be out of control in a split second it is even more so. Being able to bring this understanding about is why I so loved that job.

On the subject of driving, in 1996 Marilyn had another one of her original birthday present ideas and bought me membership of the Institute of Advanced Motorists. To be honest I had always felt a slightly sneaking disdain for their members as being mostly older gentlemen in hats and string-backed driving gloves. Well, there were still a few of them around but for the most part, those we met were very different and were an enthusiastic bunch of drivers who were genuinely interested in both their cars and their driving so once again Marilyn's intuition had proved accurate as I fitted in quite well.

Once a member I was allocated an 'observer'. This is the fully qualified member allocated to be a mentor and instructor in the skills needed for more advanced driving behaviour. Mine was David Moore who with his wife Brenda have become dear friends. The way the system worked was that David and I would arrange dates when we could go out together and he would literally 'observe' my driving and then provide feedback as to what I needed to work on.

Whilst I was very grateful for Dave's company and support, I felt on very familiar ground once I realised that the IAM system is exactly the same as the Police System of Car Control as set out in the Roadcraft handbook that I had studied way back in my early police years. This is not at all to say I didn't make any errors, most of which were probably about observing speed limits but that has always been a fault.

The System is about observation and having the car at the right speed, gear and position on the road on the approach to any hazard. If we all did that there would be no accidents because to be quite frank based on my police experience there are very few if any, true accidents. They are almost all caused by driver error of one type or another, be it excess speed or failing to notice the surrounding or developing conditions. After relatively few observer sessions which were more or less revision for me, Dave thought I was ready to take the assessment which happily I passed and so ended another little chapter although, as I said, we are still very much in touch more than twenty years later.

iii

In parallel with all this stuff for me; as a result of the chair caning course and membership of the Basket Makers Association, Marilyn had started to take an interest in basket making too, although it was indeed out of general interest rather than a serious ambition to start yet another occupation. As it happened, she found a course being run right on our doorstep at the Old Rectory private adult education centre in Fittleworth and signed up with some friends to do the course which is where they met tutor Sandra Barker, one of the country's leading lights in the basketry world. The upshot of this was that the friends decided to save the cost of attending further courses by simply running their own in their own homes and contracting Sandra in to do the teaching and the first one was arranged at the home of a friend up near Guildford.

The general view was that the idea was a great success although from where I was sitting the criteria for success was clearly open to interpretation. There was certainly some work done together with, it must be admitted, a lot of general gossip and a certain amount of wine seemed to disappear too as evidenced not just by the empty bottles but by the wonky shape of some of the baskets produced. They certainly had fun which was great and dispersed with a plan to do the next one at our place a bit later or maybe even the following year.

I'm going to digress slightly now but this story has a way to run yet.

4   AN IDEA DEVELOPS

i

Writing this now I find it hard to believe how much we packed into what was barely three years and there was quite a bit more that went on in the background beyond what I've described above. This was mostly associated with our connection to Spain that began back in '89 when Alex first came to stay.

Following on from that we had two other students who also came to our house back in Surrey. One was Silvia whose brother was a friend of Alex and who we are still in touch with today. The other was Diego from Palma in Mallorca who came twice, once to the house in Guildford and the second time when we were living in a caravan on the site of our house building project in Horsley. I remember that one day he saw a fox in the garden and being a town boy was very nervous about the 'wild animals' so close to where he was sleeping. Sadly, we lost touch with him.

We also have a Spanish friend in Farnham and through her we met students Lucea and Lorena. They wanted to stay with us but couldn't as we were by that time in Fittleworth and they ideally needed to be somewhere with a bit of life. So we arranged for them to stay with another friend near

Guildford.

The result of all this Spanish stuff was that we made a few more visits to meet their respective parents and bit by bit fell more and more in love with the country in general and Catalunya in particular. Almost imperceptibly the idea germinated that perhaps we could make a life there ourselves. Part of this was driven by our affection for the families, the appeal of the climate and the area, low property prices and the realization that with Alex's parents and their professional friends we had met we did have a ready-made support network if we decided to take the plunge.

Two other factors were also at play. One was that there was no way we saw ourselves going to a touristic area and just sliding into the ex-pat community which as far as we could see was a recipe for potential disaster. We had seen it with others including some former police colleagues. With the cheap drink and relative isolation of the ex-pats within the wider community, their lives had just become a shallow round of drinks parties around the pool or long sessions at the golf club.

There was no way we wanted that. For us, the adventure would be the integration into Spanish culture including food and drink of course but much more importantly the language and everyday life in 'real' Spain well away from the tourist and ex-pat areas. We have listened to Brits and other nationalities living there who proudly boast about how long they have lived there and *"don't speak a word of the language"*. Our only possible response is incredulity at such a wasted opportunity, but then each to their own.

The other factor in the whole equation was what we might actually do with ourselves if we made the move because we absolutely are not people who can deal with permanent holiday mode. We need to be active, interested and occupied in some purposeful way even if only on a part-time basis.

I mentioned earlier about the canteen conversations when we imagined retiring to run a bed and breakfast business. I guess most of us knew that was a bit of a daydream back then but having retired and faced with the idea of a move to Spain, some sort of accommodation business as both useful occupation and second revenue stream before the state pension arrived seemed at the very least something to consider.

As I thought more around it, I remembered my stay at the little B&B in Andalucía some years before where I'd done the language course. At that time, it has to be said the arrangements were pretty basic in terms of things like en-suite facilities and the general level and quality of fittings and so on. I said to Marilyn *"I think we could do that but we could do it so much better."*

So this was the point at which the idea of us moving to Spain and setting up accommodation to provide holiday language courses first began to emerge as conceivably possible. I don't think the question of where was ever really an issue because for all the reasons stated already about a ready-made network and so on there was never really an alternative in our minds to Catalunya. *[I will allow you dear reader to think this one through but sufficient to say that it was this one element in our otherwise quite well-considered plan that was flawed. If you think you have cracked it, make a note of why and discover later if you were right.]*

As to exactly where in Catalunya we might go to, well that was a huge issue for which we really had no answer. Obviously, we wanted it to be somewhere attractive in scenery terms but there was no shortage of possible locations so we began initially by searching the property adverts all over the region. What we did know though was that if possible, we would rather like to take on one of the old stone masias in the country, many of which were ridiculously cheap compared to UK prices for similar sized properties.

I think that at this stage we probably really did see our whole future in Spain but also decided that it would be good to have a small bolt-hole back in England for two reasons. One was that in the initial stages if anything went wrong, we would have somewhere to run to, but in the longer term once settled abroad a rentable property back here would have been a very useful extra income.

Initially, as we were living in Sussex, we thought a flat in Chichester or on the coast would be nice until by chance Marilyn happened to look at rental prices in Guildford. They were so much higher than in Sussex although the properties to buy were not that much more expensive so we focused on the Guildford area for our bolt-hole.

In the meantime, we had somehow to narrow down our search areas in Spain and set about a series of joint and solo exploration trips to different parts of Catalunya to really try to get a feel for the various regions and if possible, to actually see a few properties. Coastal areas held some attraction but were inclined to be a bit touristic for us. We wanted country but not too remote although we also thought about village properties and the benefits of easier integration with locals. Further inland, the scenery was dramatically beautiful but a bit remote from transport hubs where our potential clients would be arriving and so on and on went the various considerations.

Predictably, with us now more focused on this new plan our domestic earning activities came under threat due to our various absences but as at that time we were never away for more than a week or so we managed to disguise it quite well and keep all the various balls in the air without telling anyone what the big game plan was.

As I write this, I find it almost impossible to recall when we went to the different areas but we certainly did cover some ground and had tremendous fun meeting up with agents at plots of land or piles of rubble in the middle of nowhere. There is however one particular story that is worth telling because it too has had such far-reaching consequences.

ii

One day a little while before we were due to head off yet again but together this time, Marilyn said *"I wonder if there are any basket-makers in Catalunya."* I said *"You've got the members handbook. Have a look."*

Now it won't come as a surprise to learn that there was someone or there'd be no point to the story. Marilyn said *"There's one near Solsona. I'm going to write to him. At least it'll be another contact"* Well Solsona was interesting as it was an area we had planned to visit because it was much further inland, almost into the foothills of the Pyrenees and in the general direction of a town in the mountains called Tremp that had also caught our attention. We thought we could wrap the two together in one excursion.

A while later we had a charming letter from Lluis Grau, the basket maker, saying he would be pleased to welcome us to his home. He explained that on the day we were thinking we might be in the area he also had some other guests coming as it was his 'saint day' which the Spanish tend to celebrate like birthdays. He provided us with directions that we should follow the C55 from Cardona to the 12 km marker and then look out for a pile of stones on the left after about a hundred metres. Here we were to turn left and follow the road for about 6 km to his house which was called Rectoria de Riner.

About a week later found us out in the middle of Catalunya heading north from Cardona in a region known as Solsones due to Solsona being the major town of the area. As instructed at around 12 km we slowed down and then almost immediately saw the little cairn of pebbles beside the road at a small junction.

I said to Marilyn *"This is it then"* and made the turn onto the 'road' as Lluis had described it. Well, 'road' would have been quite a generous description because after about sixty metres the made-up surface ran out and it became a dust track barely a car's width across that snaked off into the countryside which at first was quite open but then quite quickly became pine forest.

The track became progressively worse as we continued, with deep ruts from timber vehicles and transverse gullies eroded by the run-off from the steeply sloping hillside. I wasn't overly worried, well perhaps a little but then we looked at each other and almost simultaneously said *"What on earth are we doing?"* and then collapsed into laughter.

There we were in the middle of nowhere with only a smattering of Spanish between us, heading to see a guy we didn't know from Adam. Turning wasn't an option because the track was cut into the hillside and so sloped steeply down or up on each side.

To be honest, it was a bit unnerving but we couldn't stop laughing and, in any event, had no choice but to carry on. Then we saw it. Out across the valley on a hilltop was a church tower and an adjoining stone building and behind that again a large square stone structure like some kind of fortification.

Rectoria de Riner

The penny dropped when I saw the church outline and realized that with a Rectoria (rectory) would go a church. *"That must be it."* I said., *"Look you can see the church."* So on we went and it must indeed have been best part of another two or three kilometres of twisty spine-jarring track before we found ourselves at the site.

There were a couple of stone posts one of which I think had fallen over and on a rock beside the one on our left was Lluis. He had a bundle of willow wands beside him and was working at them with a knife or that's how I remember the scene.

We pulled into the courtyard and went to meet Lluis who was smiling broadly and welcomed us in heavily accented English. He had a wonderful open face with these really smiley blue eyes and he ushered us into the huge old building through the stone arched entrance door. Lluis was a man of about my own age, so, mid 50's although a bit more weather-beaten than me from the sun I guess. He looked good though, slim and fit but above all, he had an air of serenity about him which was both disarming and infectious.

Once inside the building, its poor state of repair became more obvious. Not to put too fine a point on it the place was almost a ruin and Lluis explained that he had it rent-free on the basis that he would do some repairs. The interior was dark and smelled damp but was also very pleasantly cool compared to the heat outside.

Furnishings were rudimentary with a small stove and table and to one side a low single bed. Some of the windows were out and there was no bathroom as such. In the loo there was a WC and a bucket for flushing but as Lluis told us, not connected to anything other than the open air a bit further down the hillside. He had apparently only just put it in as we and other friends were coming.

Lluis explained that he had been a monk for many years but for various reasons felt unable to continue. So, looking for a complete change in his lifestyle he had wanted to do something with his hands and hit on the idea of basket making as it ticked the creativity box and also had minimal environmental impact. But first, he had to learn the technique; so to provide some daily bread he had come from Barcelona to Solsona which has a long history of knife making and found work assembling knives for one of the local factories.

He had a piece-work arrangement whereby the factory supplied him with the components and paid him on output. He fitted this in to provide a minimal income while he did some of the building repairs as well as seeking out local basket makers to learn their skills.

As he showed us around the place, I could see that apart from the poor condition of the building the location at around 600 metres in altitude was nothing less than idyllic with pine-clad hillsides as far as the eye could see. Located on a hill in what to us seemed the middle of nowhere, the old building and the adjoining unused church of St Martin were something of a puzzle. I couldn't understand why the church was there until Lluis explained that the 'parish' would have consisted of several very small hamlets and individual houses scattered at some distance from each other in the surrounding hills and that probably the only time they came together would be for worship that might require a journey of some distance over rough country mule tracks. With the effect of rural depopulation, the local community such as it was had almost ceased to exist and for that reason, the church was effectively redundant.

Both church and the rectoria dated from the 18th century and to my surprise have quite a lot of information about them on-line. Behind them, there was the fortified building I had also seen from a distance. Known as the Torre de Riner this former military structure with its six-metre-thick wall dates from the 10th century and is all that remains of the ancient Castel de Riner that formed part of a chain of similar fortifications across Catalunya.

(What none of us knew at that point was the devastation that would shortly come in the form of the 1998 forest fire. The wonderful forests were burnt to nothing and Lluis was lucky to escape with his life as the firestorm swept through.)

Lluis led us downhill to the river where he used an old mill and watercourse in his basketry work. He had managed to encourage some willow to grow in this damp area and had a kind of flooded basin where he soaked the wands before use. To be honest, I marvelled at his commitment and apparent contentment with this very simple, not to say basic, situation.

A short while later back up at the old house it wasn't long before the other guests appeared. There was a man Lluis introduced as Vicente that was a long-time friend from Barcelona and as I recall was an artist or perhaps a jeweller. The other was an older woman who looked just like the grandmother we would all like and came along with a large picnic basket packed with crockery and picnic food. So she was clearly aware that the catering amenities at Riner were a bit on the basic side. To say that she too was a friend from Barcelona would be to seriously understate the lady.

Her name was Teresa Roca and if you think you've seen the surname before, almost everyone who has been to Spain will have seen it in their bathrooms. This Senora Roca was no less than the owner of the huge Roca sanitary ware empire.

Not fazed in the slightest by the surroundings, Teresa set out the food in the old building and we sat down for our indoor saint's day picnic. I couldn't help smiling at the surreal situation. Here we were in the middle of nowhere; a couple of Brits who thought it might be interesting to carry on along a track to 'who knew where', an ex-monk, a Barcelona jeweller and a wealthy businesswoman all having afternoon tea in a ruin in the middle of the forest. Honestly, you couldn't make it up and it was absolutely delightful.

When it came time to go, Marilyn said to Lluis *"You must come and visit us sometime and you can meet some English basket makers."* With that, we said our goodbyes to all and wound our way back to the main road and further exploration and meetings with agents and so on. Marilyn is always sincere in what she says but she could have had no idea of where that invitation would lead. We would find out the first thing before too long.

5 STILL UNDECIDED

i

I think that by about the middle of 1997 we were fairly sure that the idea of moving to Spain could be a runner but were still pretty much afraid of taking such a big step so were both content to let it simmer for a while so to speak and get on with our lives in Fittleworth.

This meant carrying on more or less as usual and to be honest there was not a lot wrong with life as usual for us around that time. The garage and new workshop were sorted and I was getting a fair amount of handyman work or as much as I wanted. My time at the skid pan was still enjoyable and any other time was taken with the antique dealers at Petworth for whom I seemed to spend time either patching up furniture or ferrying stuff around in their van.

Marilyn had moved on a bit within the Tourist Information service and having moved to Midhurst as an assistant initially, applied for and then was appointed manager on a job share basis. The other half of the job share was taken by Brenda, wife of my IAM observer David as the couple had by then become good friends.

Thinking about the possible move to Spain I was determined to cover the issue of occupation if for some reason we didn't or were unable to get the accommodation business going and came up with the idea that even on a part-time basis I could perhaps teach English. To that end, I signed on to a course at Multi-Lingua in Guildford to learn how to teach English as a Foreign Language or TEFL as it was then known. This was seriously difficult, even for me with the training background I had in the police.

The course was a month of probably the most intensive learning I had ever done. Until then, that description applied to my instructor training course in the police some twenty years earlier but this was something else because it was so short – just a month. Fortunately for me, I already had the grammar content whereas others had to learn all that as well as the techniques involved in 'target language teaching'.

This means that from the moment you enter a class the only language anyone is allowed to utter is the target language – English in this case. It did not matter if the instructor could speak a few words of the students' mother tongue which could on occasion have been useful to explain some intricacy. The rule was 'Only English' and believe me one became very adept at explaining things in the most basic of language or by mime or drawing which frequently led to total hilarity but was a great learning method.

I could certainly see the point because as well as being a more or less 'total immersion' type of learning it was really the only workable technique as our practice classes were invariably made up of several nationalities with very different mother tongues. Anyway, in the event, I passed the course and got my TEFL certificate which would have qualified me to teach English anywhere in the world. The very day I finished the course I was offered a job in China for a year. Had I been young, free and single I would have been off like a shot. TEFL has been the passport to some fabulously interesting travel opportunities for thousands over the years. But Hey! We had our own agenda.

ii

I can't remember exactly when this happened but one day we had a letter from Lluis Grau, the basket-maker we had met and to whom Marilyn had so casually thrown out the invitation to visit us at home. The letter went something like:

"Dear Marilyn and Brian. Thank you for your invitation. I am coming to stay with you for six weeks"

Surprised was not in it. I said something like *"Bloody hell! Six weeks! Two would be fine but what on earth can we do with him for six weeks?"*

I am blessed with a wife who seems to take things pretty much as they come. We are both probably a bit less resilient now but back then things like this seemed to roll off her back. I have always reckoned it has a lot to do with when she worked for the police, taking emergency calls and had to remain unfazed no matter what.

For the same reason, she has always had a remarkable ability to cut to the chase, marshal facts and organize solutions as if it is second nature to her. *"THANK GOD FOR THAT!"* is all I can say and so she went to work.

Marilyn's original invitation had been for Lluis to come and meet some English basket makers to study their techniques and so thanks once again to the Members' Handbook in no time at all it seemed she had it all set up. Members were amazingly hospitable.

Working from our base in Sussex Marilyn arranged several visits to

makers within a day's travel which included as far afield as the Somerset Levels and where at various homes and workshops we were welcomed, shown local basketry styles and methods, fed and watered before heading off to the next port of call.

Lluis' time with us at Fittleworth coincided with the course Marilyn and her friends had planned at our house so Lluis became a bit of a star turn and was able to show them all a few of his own basketry methods from Spain.

He stayed with us for a couple of weeks and then Marilyn presented him with a carefully programmed itinerary that would take him much further afield to makers all over the country.

To cut a long story short again at this point, the trip was an unqualified success; Lluis had a great time, made many contacts and gathered a whole raft of information about English basket-making methods and a very useful network.

A few months later when we were once again going to Catalunya, we attempted to contact Lluis to arrange a call-in as we would be nearby. He said he wouldn't be at home and apologized for not meeting us because he would be in England, walking with Anna. The same thing happened again the next time we asked and in due course, Lluis explained that whilst near Birmingham he had got to know Anna Champeney, a young woman who had an interest in Spain and could speak some Spanish and so not surprisingly they had kept in contact.

We also learnt that Anna had an affinity for the Galicia region of Spain so together they had gone exploring and fallen in love. The next we heard was that they had moved to Galicia and were living happily in a beautiful region of Ourense province known as Ribeira Sacra, which means sacred riverside owing to the number of monasteries in the area.

Since moving to Galicia, Anna has become a weaver, Lluis is still a basket–maker and the most wonderful thing of all is that they have a lovely daughter called Thomasina. Talk about serendipity; none of this would have happened had Marilyn not said one day back in the 90's *"I wonder if there are any basket-makers in Catalunya"* and I had not said *"Well you've got the members handbook. Have a look."*

iii

By way of a diversion from our undecidedness, we decided that a change to our frequent travel destination was in order and around December 1997 we set off for a month to the other side of the world.

The year before Marilyn and I got together in 1983 she had been to Australia by herself as was her practice in those days. In fact, it was just before her setting out that we met in the bar at the police HQ as she was saying to a friend that she needed a camera for her trip. I offered the loan of mine which she didn't actually take up but on her return, she got in touch and asked if I'd be interested to see the photos and the rest, as they say, is history.

She had said several times over the years that she would love to do another trip together to Australia. Apart from the attraction of travel for its own sake, there were people we both wanted to see. There was an elderly couple who were friends of her parents who had gone over in the '60s as '£10 poms' on the assisted immigration scheme and were settled in the

Melbourne area. In truth, they never did really settle though and made several trips back to the UK where they stayed with Marilyn's family although the existence of a family out there always precluded a complete return to the land of their roots.

I also had a connection out in New Zealand. My one-time best friend and indeed 'best man' at my first wedding was Richard Whittingham. He'd gone off to Australia around 1979 after his second marriage had collapsed and initially made quite a success of things. When the next relationship went belly-up, he went travelling in the Far East and met with a woman he hoped to bring back to Australia. Unfortunately, she was denied entry there but was accepted in New Zealand so as a result the North Island more or less had to be added to our itinerary.

The trip was brilliant and so much more worthwhile than my bar-crawling experience in my teens. We stopped over in sultry Singapore where we marvelled at the organization and cleanliness of the place while we hopped from one cool air-conditioned location to another.

We also did the obligatory visit to Raffles Hotel and sampled the world-famous Singapore Sling cocktail in the Long Bar. And to be honest that was about the total of our experience there before we were back on board for the second leg to Aukland where I had also been with P&O.

We hired a car and travelled north via the bubbling mud and geysers of Rotorua to Bay of Islands where we found Richard and his Asian partner Aileen. They were living in a bungalow of sorts that Richard was in the process of creating from a former double garage. Between them, they had set up an office cleaning business which was going well and just confirmed the 'comeback kid' label we had attached to him following his recovery from previous setbacks. They made us very welcome and took us around to see a few of the local tourist sights and a few lesser-known but interesting places. Sadly, our time with them was quite short and we set off again to Australia.

Not that he knew it then, but Richard was going to need every bit of his 'comeback' ability within the next few months. Probably about nine months later I heard from him that Aileen had gone. Apparently, she took off to see her sick father in Hong Kong but only after she left did Richard discover that she had emptied their bank accounts. He never heard from her again.

We had a great time in Australia but of course in the limited days available could barely scratch the surface of the vast and fascinating country. We stayed briefly with the friends in Melbourne before flying up to Ayers Rock in the Red Centre where we suffered swarms of flies while waiting for a sadly rather cloudy sunrise over the rock. It was very atmospheric though and just one of those things you have to do.

On her previous trip, Marilyn had covered huge distances by Greyhound bus and while we could now afford to take the faster aerial route, she said that I really should do at least one trip across the Outback by bus to truly get an impression of the place.

We took the bus for the six-hour (460 km) trip from Ayers Rock to Alice Springs and she was absolutely right. Nothing prepares one for the vast emptiness of central Australia and it was certainly worth doing. A very funny thing happened on the journey though. We were about an hour out of Alice when the driver announced (you have to imagine the accent) *"We might have a bit of a hold up near Alice as the road's flooded"* I couldn't believe my ears. We're in one of the driest places on the planet and the road is flooded! The Todd River that runs through Alice is almost always just a dry bed but from time to time a storm in the nearby hills produces a flash flood of water that can fill the river in literally just a few minutes.

"So what happens now?" we chorused. *"Oh no worries."* he says. *"We just wait until it's gone. If it takes a while they'll bring a chopper out with some food and a few*

beers to keep us going." In the event, the chopper wasn't needed as the water apparently came and went – if there is not a lot it just soaks into the ground and disappears or if the flow is prolonged it eventually joins the Hale River and flows into Lake Eyre.

Now, this could only happen in Australia. Known as 'Henley on Todd', there is a very ironic regatta – yes regatta, on the Todd River each year where competitors get into bottomless boats and race by running along the dry river bed. I kid you not – look it up on-line. Apparently, it attracts huge crowds to what is an important event – so important that the regatta is insured against rain.

There were other fascinating attractions in Alice Springs that included the Flying Doctor Service and The School of the Air, both of which exist due to the huge distances between settlements of population and individual homesteads or cattle stations. The Telegraph Station is now a museum but was established in 1872 to re-transmit telegraph messages by Morse Code between Adelaide and Darwin.

There was so much more we could have seen and done on this trip but time was limited so our last stop was Sydney with its iconic bridge and Opera House that I had actually seen before when there with P&O.

Our stop-over on the homeward leg was in Kuala Lumpur, Malaysia where we gazed awestruck at the recently completed Petronas Twin Towers that until 2004 were the tallest buildings on the planet. In KL we were also met by friends of my sister who kindly entertained us in their home and took us on an excursion to Malacca a coastal town on the narrow straits between the Malay Peninsular and the Indonesian island of Sumatra. This area is the principal 'short cut' between the Pacific and Indian Oceans so is both commercially and strategically important as well as being a popular haunt of modern marine pirates.

While our Australian trip had been an enjoyable experience, we were both aware that it was really only a diversion from the main issue exercising our minds and that was the need to either forget the whole idea or to firmly bite the bullet and make some more positive moves to further the idea of a move to Spain.

6 SEARCH FOR A NEW HOME

i

Our trips to Catalunya continued during 1998 and between us, either alone or together, we spent weeks out there meeting agents with a variety of results, none of which produced the future home of our dreams or at least none that we could afford.

We were shown everything from reasonably up together country houses and masias that were too expensive to those needing *'reformaciones'* (refurbishment). In some cases, these amounted to little more than a pile of rubble in a field. We asked about water supplies and in one place Marilyn was shown a damp patch of ground nearby that was apparently a perfect *'fuente'* (spring). We looked at a former *'molino'* (water mill) that was clearly the subject of serious periodic flooding judging from the amount of driftwood in the basement and were told we could easily *'desviar el rio'* (divert the river!!).

House-hunting in another country is a completely different ball-game if one is not buying a new white painted box in one of the many coastal hot spots. It's necessary to accept that in the countryside, which was mostly where we were looking, you have to suspend our notion of 'normal', one element of which is that normal services may not be present. Such was the case with both water and sewage services and it wasn't long before the idea of a spring or a *'fossa septica'* (septic tank) became perfectly acceptable.

It was also a great way to learn more vocabulary beyond the holiday Spanish needed to get a beer and a paella. There is an excellent dictionary called the 'Oxford-Duden Pictorial Spanish-English Dictionary' that provides labelled illustrations of anything you could possibly need to know. In our case 'how to tap a spring', which gave chapter and verse on the process of turning a damp patch of ground into a usable water supply together with a diagram and a complete list of all the materials and components required. It is truly one of the most useful and informative books I've ever read. Almost bedtime reading in fact – well maybe for a techno-nerd like me.

At this time we were casting our search pretty widely including the far south of Catalunya close to the border with Valencia province which was an area we had been introduced to by Alex's parents. They had even taken us down there on one occasion to a fiesta in Vincent's home village and also on a bit of a tour around the area including Deltebre which is a town, as the name suggests, that sits within the vast wetland area of the Ebro delta.

It was a very different landscape there, especially when compared to the more mountainous areas inland that we had been considering. Not without its attractions though as it is on the coast which we felt quite a number of our potential clients would like. It is also an area that is highly popular with naturalists of varied interests, anglers and artists to name just a couple. A particular feature is the vast areas of rice that are grown there along with the lagoon, sand spits and offshore island.

We had seen a few houses advertised in the region so set off again on another occasion with appointments to meet a couple of agents. At the airport, the strangest thing happened. As we walked to the aircraft and looked up, on the nose was the plane's name – "Delta d'Ebre". Was this an omen? Whatever; it was seriously weird.

This trip is always remembered as the 'yellow trousers trip' because the agent we had arranged to meet appeared in a pair of bright yellow trousers. This was a good time before Michael Portillo appeared on our screens in his gaudy collection of jackets and trousers and quite frankly back then we felt that someone who was trying to sell us a house should have been more seriously attired. Just shows how staid we were I guess.

The houses we saw were a bit of a mixed bag although the common theme was the large plots that went with each. It wasn't uncommon down there for a property to be sitting on a couple of acres planted with olives and oranges plus a decent sized garden and a variety of outbuildings. At first of course it can be very exciting to be offered so much for your money especially when compared to property prices here in the UK.

However, it is important to keep taking reality checks around such things as the amount of physical work it is going to take to keep the land in order, who will be pruning the grapes and fruit trees, how far is it to get a bottle of milk and so on and this can bring one up a bit sharply.

Irrigation was another issue if one had any inclination to serious gardening. Some houses already had systems installed and others not which would have been a major expense.

However, of the several properties that 'yellow trousers' showed us, there was one with distinct possibilities. It was in very good order, had all the accommodation we needed as a home and for our business ideas and had a beautifully prolific and irrigated plot. The only downside was that it was right on a fairly main road. We did give it serious consideration though, but in the end, decided against it. Not that we could have made a firm offer anyway because we still had not sold the house at Fittleworth although we had realised by that time that houses out there moved pretty slowly and there was every chance it would still be available once we were 'cash in hand' buyers.

One of the agents we hooked up with was quite a character and chattered away in rapid machine-gun Spanish almost continually apparently confident we understood every word which of course we didn't. We did at one point get to talk about Spanish culture and a bit about how modern attitudes might be affecting gender issues in the country especially considering the rather macho image outsiders have of Spanish men. Now if that sounds as though our Spanish was competent, believe me it wasn't, but somehow we got the gist of a lot of it with one particular exception.

This was when he wanted to tell us a joke and as we were clearly not picking up the punch line he resorted to mime. We had more or less understood that although in Spain men tended to see themselves as head of the house the reality was rather different. But getting the joke was so hard for us and frustrating for him. His antics were hilarious though and it wasn't long before all three of us were almost helpless with laughter.

He started by walking a few steps and miming the opening of a door and we managed to pick up '*en casa*' which means 'at home'. Next, he mimed what looked like he was flapping his arms in an attempt to take off which is what really started the laughing. We couldn't get it at all although we picked up the word *'chacqueta'*, which we didn't know but eventually cottoned on that he was taking off of a coat or 'jacket'. Ok. Got it thus far.

His next move was the funniest. With both hands, he grabbed at the crotch of his trousers, raised his hands up and thrust them out in front of him accompanied by a word that sounded like *'kahonies'* which we had never heard. Time and again he went through this charade as we all lapsed into progressively more helpless hysteria.

Another word we picked up was *'cuelgan'* which we didn't recognize at first. Eventually, we realised that he wasn't saying *'kahonies'* but *'cajones'*, which we understood as 'drawers' and we also thought *'cuelgan'* had something to do with hanging but still just couldn't quite see what he meant and, in the end, we had to give it up and put it down to just another one of those funny stories we took home from Spain.

It was probably a couple of months later when we were once again in Spain and visiting Alex's family in Barcelona and I was telling his father Vincent about our estate agent and his mime. He got it immediately, started laughing and then he explained.

The guy was not saying *'cajones'* but *'cojones'* the slang word for balls as in testicles. The expression he was attempting to mime to us was that in Spain the men may think they are in charge but in reality, when they go indoors, they 'hang their balls up with their jacket.'

What it did emphasise however was the care needed with spelling and pronunciation of some words to avoid getting into serious trouble. It's the same with typing that we all do so much more of these days. I do a lot of photography and often write about this or that 'shot'. I am super careful to always read anything before hitting the send button as the *i* and the *o* are next door on the keyboard. Think about it.

By late 1998 we had seen a lot of properties including a few that could possibly have worked for our idea but of course, we didn't have the funds to make any firm offers. This forced us back to the realisation that if we were serious about this idea our house needed to go on the market. However, this was a bit 'chicken and egg' in that we couldn't really embark on the project without selling up which would mean we would have nowhere to live so we decided that stage one would have to be the sale of Wingates in Fittleworth and the purchase of the flat mentioned previously.

Actually, this happened surprisingly fast and it seemed like no time at all before we were no longer the owner of our '*Shangri-La*' half-acre in West Sussex but living in a two-bedroom flat at Shalford near Guildford albeit with quite a few thousand in the bank. At one level we felt quite bereft in the flat with just a fraction of our total possessions but at the same time, there was a real feeling of liberation with all our 'stuff' away in storage. Once settled in the flat we were free to go house-hunting in Catalunya.

As Marilyn wasn't working, we were able to go together more often although not every time because we still had things going on at home for either one of us and the cost of kenneling our little Benjy was a bit of an issue especially as he wasn't too well either. We soon came to the conclusion that as we had now taken the first step we might as well really get serious about it and that it would be easier if we tried to find somewhere to rent out there so that we could continue or search together.

Among our preparations for transferring our whole life to Spain, the question of the actual removal had to be considered and quotes obtained. Make no mistake, we were deadly serious and even planned to take my little grey Fergie tractor which in our mind's eye we saw ourselves using to cultivate our new 'Shangri-La' plot under the Spanish sun.

We didn't imagine that a removal firm would undertake to transport a tractor and were considering that we might have to do it ourselves by trailer. In fact, in a lighter moment, we even joked about perhaps driving it down while towing a little old caravan like a couple of travellers and imagined what a hoot it would be. Not exactly very realistic but would probably have made us famous across France. These days we could do it as a sponsored event and make a fortune for a charity while having fun. Now, there's a thought.

Anyway, the removal guys were not in the least fazed by the proposition and simply explained they had moved such things before and it would be no problem. So that was the plan that would come into effect once we had found our new green acre and were ready for the full removal.

In March '99 Marilyn was again out in Catalunya prospecting on her own when her father was taken ill. We had only seen him a couple of days before she left and spent a pleasant time together but just a few days later he went down with a sudden and severe chest infection and was whisked into hospital. Marilyn changed a flight to make an early return but by the time she arrived her father was no longer conscious. As is often the case with elderly people the infection was overwhelming and the prognosis was as bad as it could be. Sadly, he died a couple of days later.

Our poor little dog Benjy had been off-colour for a few months with a heart murmur but appeared to be managing reasonably well and so was included in the planned expedition. As any pet owner will understand, knowing when the time has come for a much-loved family friend is an almost impossible task. However, around Easter '99 his progressive heart failure became more difficult for him and his quality of life that the decision was made for us and fortunately before we were actually underway. A very sad moment but merciful in that it happened while we were still here.

All in all, the spring of '99 was not a happy time and, in many ways, it was good that we had other issues to focus on by way of a diversion.

It was about mid-summer when I struck gold and found a super place to rent in an ideal location. It was a modern furnished townhouse over three levels and I thought it would be perfect as a base to live whilst we pursued our search. I called Marilyn and she agreed to come out straight away. Once she saw it, we decided it would ideally suit our purpose and agreed on the rental before going home to arrange things for the grand departure.

L'Esquirol was a rural village in the foothills of the Pyrenees, and about an hour inland from both Girona and Barcelona so we felt the area worked well as far as our future potential clients were concerned. The village's full name at the time we were there was Santa Maria de Corco – L'Esquirol. This double-barreled mouthful had an interesting origin. As you might guess *esquirol* means squirrel in both Catalan and Spanish but is also a pejorative term for a strike-breaker or 'scab' as might be said in English. The story goes that in the 19th century striking textile workers in the nearby town of Manlleu were replaced by workers from Santa Maria de Corco after which the word was added to the original village name in colloquial usage. So established had this become that quite recently in 2014 it was officially renamed simply L'Esquirol.

I had better pause here as we are not even there yet and I'm in danger of getting carried away.

ii

So, to say *"We're going to move to Spain."* is one thing but the actual doing of it is something else again. Not least of which is breaking the news to friends and family that this much talked of idea is not fantasy but really is about to happen.

I'm not sure that anyone actually believed we would do it but their sense of reality changed dramatically when we booked our two ferry crossings. The first was for a trip I was planning to make with a friend in a hired van to get a load of our essential equipment like the home computer, clothing, personal effects and a few other 'must-have' items down in advance of our own removal.

The second thing that clearly reinforced our serious intent was the purchase of a left-hand drive car.

This was surprisingly easy; as it turned out that there is a major left-hand drive dealer in Basingstoke. Well, no car purchase is ever really a good deal but at least we were able to part exchange our existing saloon for a more spacious Peugeot estate car. Driving the left-hander certainly took a bit of getting used to here in England but at least it wasn't going to be for very long.

So that was it. It was barely six weeks after I'd found the house in L'Esquirol that we found ourselves saying our goodbyes and setting out for our drive through France to what we firmly intended would be our new long-term life in Spain running an accommodation business.

PART TWO

SPAIN

7 L'ESQUIROL

i

Occupying an elevated position at almost 700 metres, the village overlooks the extensive plain of Vic, the major town of the area.

The Plaza Major (main square) in Vic.

Apart from a rich historical and cultural heritage as one of Catalunya's most important towns, Vic is famous for its gastronomy, chief of which is the manufacture of pork products. Superb though they are, a distinct downside to this is that the whole area is pervaded with the rich smell of pig manure which is almost continuous in any part of the plain apart from when the wind blows and shares it with the surrounding area. The region is also susceptible to persistent mist across the plain which somehow seems to intensify or trap the piggy smell. We called it the 'pig poo fog'. Curiously one does kind of get accustomed to it, almost (but not quite) missing its heady aroma on leaving the area.

The village had a couple of bars and several small shops including a mini-market, a butcher, baker, greengrocer, electrical/DIY and right next door to us was a wonderful bakery and cake shop run by our new neighbours and soon-to-be friends Dolors and husband Santi the master baker. Directly opposite there was a small *hostal* (the Spanish spelling) that also had a very good restaurant and bar that we made frequent use of and quite quickly got to know the owners Lluis and Cecelia.

Our balcony was above the van so the smell from the adjoining bakery was wonderfully mouthwatering.

Inside the flat

From the outset, we were made to feel welcome although also regarded with a fair level of quiet curiosity which was easy to intuit although never expressed with a direct question like "*What are you two doing here?*" While we weren't about to tell everyone we came in contact with what our plan was, people that we became closer to like the bakery couple and the *hostal* owners opposite were made party to our intentions and clearly, that information got distributed through the local grapevine. As a result, it wasn't long before silent curiosity was replaced with information about where there might be a house to buy or rent.

The language issue was interesting too. By this time our halting Spanish was improving, and if not exactly to a fluent conversational level we were able to make ourselves well understood in the local shops and so on and initially the locals responded to us in Spanish. However, after we had been in the village quite a short time, responses started coming back to us in Catalan and where we made the effort to use the odd Catalan word it was obviously appreciated.

Catalan is an identifiably separate language which, whilst similar in many ways to Castillian Spanish is far from being just a dialect. Historically the present Catalunya extended north of the Pyrenees as Greater Catalonia and the language also owes a lot of its origin to the ancient Occitan language of south-west France. A high proportion of people in Catalunya feel strongly that they could and should be independent of Spain and part of this sentiment is expressed by the prominence given to the Catalan language. Understandable when one learns how the culture of this region was oppressed during the Franco years and people were imprisoned for speaking it.

Whilst our language was more than adequate to get us around the shops and restaurant, seek directions and similar activity, renting a house took us into a new range of vocabulary when the odd thing started to go wrong. One of which was the domestic boiler (*caldera*) and the situation was not eased by the fact that our landlady stubbornly persisted in speaking Catalan.

Fortunately, the plumber (*fontanero*) was more amenable and agreed to explain to her that the pump (*bomba*) was defective and "*Oh by the way Senora, your oil storage drums (bidones) are now illegal since the latest change in the plumbing and central heating (calefaccion) regulations*" You might imagine how that went down – her new tenants were obliging her to spend money. She did pay up of course but not with very good grace.

Getting a telephone installed was another challenge. We could have managed with mobile phones but at some cost and we needed a land-line for an internet connection. Telefonica was the local equivalent to BT and pretty much had the monopoly on the home phone market although like here in the UK other players were emerging at that time. Telefonica was almost impossible to deal with and it was well-nigh impossible to speak English to anyone and whilst our halting Spanish was Ok 'face to face' a telephone call is far more difficult.

It was weeks of pestering before we got the line in and then only on the very day that we had more or less decided to give up the idea and continue with the 'internet café' option.

In the meantime, we were starting to explore our surroundings and getting to know the area reasonably well and to some extent, the urgency of frenzied house-hunting went slightly onto the back burner whilst we enjoyed this familiarization process.

Lying just off the road from Vic to Olot; L'Esquirol is on the road to one other place only, the stunningly picturesque village of Tavertet. This lovely little hamlet which in reality has now become more a visitor attraction than a working village perches at some nine hundred metres atop sheer precipices that drop dramatically to the valley floor and the Sau reservoir.

To get a true impression of how dramatic a location it is just Google Tavertet – images and prepare to be amazed. Fortunately, the village is being well preserved with sensitive restoration but very limited development permitted. Today it is less of a working village and many of the homes are weekenders for city folk while several others have been arranged as very nice rural guest houses or rustic restaurants although the prices are far from rustic.

One day while exploring near Tavertet we came across a wonderfully atmospheric old masia (Catalan farmhouse) that was in the early stages of restoration with workmen on site. Characterised by their heavy mellow stone walls and low-pitched roofs, masias come in many shapes and sizes from quite humble structures to some seriously impressive and vast Señorial (noble) houses. They were the type of property that we had in mind to buy if we could find one suitable. The one at Tavertet fell into the 'impressively noble' but not vast category but was the more impressive for its stunning views, being close to the edge of the cliff from where the views went on forever, frequently above the clouds.

It turned out that the house belonged to the journalist and former MP Matthew Parris and his sister and its restoration is the subject of his book A Castle in Spain. It is now operated by Matthew's sister Belinda as a 'Casa Rural' (the Spanish way of saying rustic B&B) and known as L'Avenc de Tavertet. Also worth a quick look on-line to get a true impression of what they have achieved.

Returning to the area a few years later, we spent a lovely night there and ran into the very charming Matthew Parris over coffee in the kitchen as he rushed in and out whilst completing his latest Times submission. (What a name-dropper I am).

The un-restored masia – L'avenc de Tavertet

This is l'Avenc showing the former outbuilding converted to guest cottages.

In the same area and below the cliffs of Tavertet is the Panta de Sau. *Panta* is the Catalan word for reservoir and Sau the name of the valley and village that was inundated behind the dam. There are great views to be had over the reservoir and surrounding cliffs from the Vic Parador that lies more or less at the head of the valley. Say what one likes about the Franco era, one thing he did do was to ensure that Spain's very seasonal rainfall was captured behind a huge number of dams for both drinking water and hydro-electric schemes. Spain is so mountainous that it was relatively easy to dam the river valleys to create hundreds of huge reservoirs. There are fifty in Catalunya alone.

One day while sipping a coffee on the terrace at the Vic Parador we noticed that there appeared to be a church tower out in the middle of the reservoir and discovered that it is the Romanesque church of Sant Roma de Sau that appears when the water level drops a bit.

On another occasion when the water was even lower the whole church was exposed and to our amazement, we could see that it appeared to be under restoration works. "*How weird*" we thought until someone explained that the restoration was being done so that there would still be something for the tourists to peer at below the water from the little boats that did the 'Visit the Sunken Village' tour. Very canny the Catalans.

The sunken church being repaired. As it is usually well under the water one has a very clear idea of how low the water level was then.

ii

Apart from Vic our next largest nearby town was Manlleu. An unremarkable but pleasant working town, it lies on the River Ter and boasts a particularly attractive square enclosed by arched colonnades ideally suited to taking a shady morning coffee or beer.

In common with the majority of Spanish towns we ever visited (of which there were very many) the *Plaza Major* or main square is pretty much where it all happens and on one morning in particular when we casually wandered in for a coffee it was indeed all going on.

There was the most mouth-watering smell of roasting meat wafting on the breeze, the bunting was out in abundance and a temporary dance floor had been set up beside which a country and western group were belting out a lot of familiar standards as well as stuff we didn't know. However, the funniest thing in a country famed for its Flamenco, Pasa Doble and the Sardanas folk dancing in Catalunya, was the team of line dancers complete with cowboy boots and tasselled shirts strutting and stomping loudly on the wooden floor.

A few moments of rather gob-smacked looking around soon spotted the signs telling us that we had wandered into the annual *Cerdo y Cerveza* (pork and beer) fiesta. The delicious smell was coming from a huge open fire pit of glowing embers over which no less than three whole pigs were being spit-roasted (definitely not a long life-expectancy for pigs around here) and tables had been hauled out from the bars into the colonnade for the service of beer.

Still somewhat non-plussed, we were just more or less coming to terms with this fascinating vista when we were startled by the sound of some seriously loud engines which I identified immediately as V8 motors. We turned around to see an impressive cavalcade of superbly presented American cars arriving and parking in neat echelon rows to almost fill the road around a little more than two sides of the square. The variety was amazing and included everything from some real 1950's classics through extreme and outlandish stock cars and trucks that were almost dragsters to some seriously expensive and exotic modern performance cars. It turned out that this was The American Car Club of Catalunya if you can imagine that such a thing could even exist. Their arrival was precisely choreographed because once the last vehicle had parked all the engines were revved up in unison so that the very air itself vibrated against our chests before they switched off into total silence and then a great round of applause erupted around the square.

The Spanish seem to have a delightfully refreshing disregard for rules. I found this irritating at first, coming as we did from such a buttoned-up and legally controlled environment as we have here. It was clear that parking rules, whilst they existed according to the displayed notices, were clearly of little importance and were enthusiastically ignored as were the approach zones to pedestrian crossings that we so conscientiously observe in the UK. Our initial impression of driving in Spain was that they were all mad but not so. They are almost all fast drivers and impatient of hold-ups but in the whole of our time there we saw little evidence of accidents in and around towns. Where there certainly were problems was on the fast National routes and motorways especially at weekends and the many public holidays, when the accident rate soared along sadly with the fatalities.

Curiously, for all their impatience and fast driving, not many Spanish drivers are what I would call 'good' in terms of their observation and planning. Tootling along at ordinary (but not slow) sight-seeing speeds we frequently found local drivers would come haring up behind us and then start tail-gating in their apparent anxiety to get past. There could be a straight road ahead with clear views and no double lines and still they often would not pass until we slowed or almost pulled off the road. We're used to it now and usually ignore them.

Another thing we found quite shocking was the apparent disregard for what we have come to think of as Health and Safety issues. I'm not sure if there is even an equivalent phrase in Spain. This is particularly obvious with fiestas of which there are very many. I mean imagine the risk assessment requirement here and cries of *"No Way"* if anyone suggested allowing a herd of panicking bulls to run through the public streets and then encouraged any macho young guy who fancied his chances to jump in and run along with them or try to pull the odd tail or two. You can see this in Pamplona every July.

L'Esquirol was not without its fiesta's either and one of them happened a month or so after we arrived. We were sitting in the apartment late one evening when we heard a rhythmic drumming sound getting closer and louder. We had a balcony overlooking the street but when we went to look out the whole place was in darkness as the street lights had been turned off and all we could get was the eerie sound of the relentless drumming. After a short time as the drums got even louder, we began to see a glow of lights from further down the street and then the 'devils' appeared around a corner into our street with showers of fire and sparks cascading and flying around all over.

What looked like twenty or more black-clad figures were painted with white luminous skeletons and as they danced and pranced to the drumbeat, they carried their devil's pitchforks mounted with fireworks of various descriptions. These included huge 'Catherine wheels' that spun over their heads shedding sparks all over the place including the dancers themselves. This fiesta was the Dance of the Devils and as with most similar events in Spain is essentially an historic religious day high-jacked by the fun brigade. These "fire runs" or *correfocs* as they are called in Catalunya appear at the slightest opportunity and can be found as a component of the numerous fiestas all over the country.

You have to give it to the Spanish; they certainly do know how to party and at a completely different level to us rather staid Brits. It's in this context too that health and safety issues seem to get shoved far back on the agenda. For example, in the event just described there were several cars parked along the street and these were literally and liberally showered with the fiery fall-out from the pyrotechnics. And who cared? No-one apparently.

Fire and fireworks seem to play a big part in Spanish celebrations and the father of all the events surely has to be the fiesta of San Juan on 23rd June that is almost certainly a Christian adoption of the pagan mid-summer solstice festivities. These days it is the feast of the birthday of St John the Baptist and seems to be celebrated with as much fire as possible. All over the country, huge bonfires are lit at midnight and as the flames subside people of all ages can be seen leaping over the fires. Three leaps and you are apparently purified that's if you don't fall in and end up in the hospital. Health and Safety – What's that?

This difference between the Spanish and English idea of a good night out was brought home to us when we were saying to a neighbour in L'Esquirol that it was after midnight when we heard the local kids coming back to the village on their 'motos'. *"No"* they explained. *"They were just going out."* Made us feel a bit out of it I must admit.

We concluded that if there was a choice in Spain between funding road repairs or buying *piroténicos* the fireworks would win hands down. They are a very 'heart-over-head' race and I love them. That said Catalan people are also known for their shrewd business acumen which surely accounts for the considerable wealth and economic prosperity of the province and their conviction that they could 'go it alone' independently of Spain.

iii

We did an awful lot of exploring in search of potential homes around this part of Catalunya using L'Esquirol as a base and also ventured a good bit further afield on trips that took us away for several days at a time.

One day we were in a pretty rural town called Tremp that we had found when we continued through Solsona after meeting Lluis the first time. Located in the Pyrenees amidst stunning mountain scenery it was about 180 km from Barcelona and realistically a bit too far for our likely clientele but *"what the hell"*, we liked it and this was where we made our first offer to buy a property.

It was owned by an English guy and occupied a lovely elevated site of several acres planted with olives and fruit trees and the views were to die for. We decided that the price was right, it had the accommodation we needed and despite the distance from airports, we felt that the more intrepid 'Lonely Planet' travellers would probably fall for it as we had.

There was a swimming pool full of water and on the day we visited the gardens were being watered by sprinkler. It was idyllic so we made an offer which was not rejected out of hand but the owner said he needed to think about it.

About an hour later we were talking it over excitedly in a bar when it began to dawn on us that we had been rather seduced by the overall set-up and had perhaps not pursued enough of the detail. Then almost together we said *"What did he say about the water supply?"* and neither of us could remember so this became the number one question for our visit when we went back the next day.

I can't now recall the exact words but it went something along the lines that *"Everything's fine."* More detailed questions elicited that the water came from a spring. *"Oh, that's Ok"* we thought; until he explained the spring was not on his land but on an adjoining plot that was not occupied and the owner of which was unknown. Also, he told us that the water came through a garden hose on the surface of the ground and was used to fill a dry well on his property that served as a reservoir from which he pumped his own supply.

As Tremp was in the mountains we asked about the hosepipe freezing which he agreed it did sometimes, and the only other slight inconvenience was when sheep either stood on the pipe or chewed a hole in it. We also asked about the swimming pool and sprinkler and he said that it came from a small spring on his own land but was also honest enough to say that it was seasonal and often dried up after long dry periods.

On balance we decided it was too risky especially as we were considering an accommodation business with clients who would probably want frequent showers and expect reliable amenities. It was certainly a lovely place so it was with regret we withdrew our offer and left to continue our search.

Frankly, it was just as well it turned out that way because if the offer had been accepted; rather like in Scottish law, the deal would have been binding and short of doing a runner out of the country there would have been no way out of it. What is it they say about the 'clue being in the name'? Had we been less carried away with our excitement about the place and paid closer attention to the map that brought us there we would have seen the region labelled as Mont Sec.

Another property we looked at quite close to Vic was a huge masia that was for rent rather than sale. It had not been modernized at all and one thing that stands out in my memory is the kitchen which was huge and medieval. A vast cavern of a place, the key feature was the enormous open fireplace with pot hooks and a kind of crane that was used to swing pots over the fire. Interesting and characterful it may have been and indeed would have provided a huge talking point for guests. However, practical in modern terms it was not and coupled with the need for bathrooms and additional loos it made the prospect of taking it on challenging to say the least. Although not overly expensive, the repairing lease placed a substantial burden on the tenants as the place required work and it would have needed quite a lot of money spent to bring even a part of it up to a standard we could have happily offered to our clients.

We had allocated money for whatever refurbishments would be needed and also for creating comfortable guest accommodation so that in itself was not such a problem. We were also attracted by the fact that a rental property would not at a stroke consume all our capital. However, that illusion came to an end when we discovered that whilst the initial rent was not excessive, we would be locked in for five years at a time. Also, once the owner could see us developing a successful business, he would be able to increase the rent to whatever level he wished so that was another fantasy up in smoke and almost certainly just as well.

There were a few other properties we went to see and now in hindsight, we do laugh at one or two things we actually considered. One of these was a long three-storey factory building. The ground floor was full of machinery and it was huge. I can't believe what we were thinking of, even to be considering it, apart perhaps from the ridiculously cheap price.

We stood there realistically talking about taking the top floor off, rendering it all to cover the ugly red bricks and thinking about how many bedrooms we might create. We were totally away with the fairies that day. Fortunately, we came-to in time and got back in the car.

We covered many hundreds of miles all over the province and to be honest, except for the one in Tortosa that was too close to the road and the one in Tremp we actually offered on then withdrew there was nothing that we fell in love with or that piqued our interest enough to be a contender. We were also realizing that despite all the properties we had seen online from the UK when you got to them in the flesh they just didn't measure up, but I guess it was ever thus with house-hunting.

It would have been towards the end of November or early December of 1999 that the crunch came for us when an agent bluntly told us that on our budget we weren't going to get anywhere as things had quite suddenly changed dramatically and the market was literally 'on-fire' with buyers and prices were soaring.

What had happened was that the rumour mill was circulating a report that Spaniards would not have so long to convert their pesetas that had been dual currency with the Euro since January '99. As there were zillions of pesetas in '*dinero negro*' hidden away under beds a panic ensued to launder the illegal money and one major way was by the purchase of property. The agent explained he had clients who didn't just want a property but as many as he could find them. He more or less told us "*You've got no chance unless you can find a lot more money.*"

Well, we weren't that brave or foolhardy. We had a plan and a budget that we were sure could have worked when we first started looking at places but there was no way we could go in with another £50 or £60,000 that would have been needed.

There were areas in other parts of Spain such as out in the provinces of Castilla La Mancha, Extremadura or Galicia where the property was still very cheap but to be honest, we had expended so much time and imagination on the Catalunya area and simply didn't have the energy or resolve to up sticks and start again somewhere else. Regretfully we decided to accept the adventure was over.

I felt we had failed and despite friends and family saying encouraging things like *"At least you gave it a go"* or *"You'd have felt terrible if you had never tried."* etc. the sense of defeat was absolute especially at first.

It was going to take a while to arrange our departure and return to the UK and it couldn't be achieved before Christmas so we determined to use the last couple of weeks as positively as possible.

This included even more exploring but without the house-hunting agenda so we were more or less back in holiday mode, and our sense of defeat began to lift even more as we turned our minds towards the future and what our next moves would be once we got back home.

Christmas was spent with Alex's family down in Barcelona and although it is not celebrated in quite the same way as in England it was lovely to be with the family who had become such close and supportive friends. Their disappointment was almost as acute as our own but they agreed that our decision was prudent and probably correct, all things considered.

We were still in L'Esquirol when 1999 became 2000 and remembering how New Year is welcomed at home in England, we headed off down into Vic shortly before midnight expecting to welcome the next millennium with crowds in the Plaza Major.

We couldn't have been more wrong. The place was deserted apart from one single policeman who had probably drawn the short straw and found himself on patrol instead of seeing in the New Year by eating the twelve grapes at home with his family.

Returning to the flat in L'Esquirol, we turned on the TV and watched the recordings of New Year fireworks around the world – everywhere in fact apart from Vic or L'Esquirol.

However, we didn't miss out entirely on the seasonal festivities because in Spain the greater fiesta is reserved for the celebration of *Los Reyes Magos* or The Three Kings on the 6th January, the day we know as Epiphany or Twelfth Night.

In Spain, this is the day for present giving and the day when everyone does indeed turn out into the main squares across the country to see the kings arrive in their fabulously decorated floats and wonderfully ornate 'royal' outfits casting hundreds of sweets (*caramelos*) to the children and adults alike.

It was a good final memory and we returned to the UK the next week.

A few pages back I asked you to think about where our theory was flawed and am wondering if you've seen the one small crack in our plan.

Well, it is to do with the language. When I described the course I attended all those years ago in Andalucía I mentioned how we were sent off to practice our newly acquired language on the locals.

It was our plan in offering 'Holiday Spanish Language Courses' to adopt the same idea in Catalunya. Given what I've said about the strength of the Catalan tongue our students would have had a bit of a shock had they gone out expecting to be surrounded by the Spanish language and been nonplussed as we were at being replied to in Catalan. Did you spot it? We didn't until we thought about it afterwards. Does emphasise how thorough business planning should be though.

Our few months in Catalunya were such fun and a great adventure, but clearly our holiday language course idea was never meant to be. We do often wonder how it would have worked out. It might have been a hugely successful 'happy ever after' venture with us making loads of money and wishing we had done it earlier. Equally, we could have struggled for a few years and then when the crash or '*la crisis*' struck in 2007-08 we could have been stuck there unable to sell and with no clients. We'll never know of course but to be honest we've done a lot of good stuff back here in England. And as you'll learn as we go on, future activities owe more than a little to the Spanish connection and our ideas around the provision of accommodation.

PART THREE

THE SURREY HILLS

8 THE NEXT MOVE

i

So, January 2000, the new millennium and back in the flat at Shalford. *"What's the next move?"* was the big question.

We had obviously talked about this and concluded that our priority should be to get our money back into UK property as quickly as possible. So to that end, we lost no time in getting a valuation for the flat and registering with agents to see what was out there on the market that we might like and more importantly could afford.

The first and very welcome surprise was that the flat had increased quite significantly in value in the few short months we'd owned it and looked as though it was going to more or less fund our little adventure and leave us in roughly the same financial position we were in after selling Wingates.

Although we had enjoyed our five years in Sussex, we are both Surrey people and of course very familiar with the area around Guildford so that was where in the first instance we focused our new programme of house-hunting.

The flat sold very quickly to a man who wanted it as an investment property although initially, he intended using it for his son who was going to attend Surrey University later in the year. Once the deal was agreed he wasn't in any hurry to get us out which made our search much more relaxed.

It wasn't long before some details came through the door about a house in Peaslake which is a pretty village in the Surrey Hills about eight miles from both Guildford and Dorking.

I hardly knew the area although had visited once some years before when working in the police press office and used the village constable Len West for a publicity photograph.

We went to have a look and frankly, I wasn't impressed. It was a 1930's bungalow that had been given a loft conversion to provide a further bedroom and shower a few years previously and more recently had been the subject of further refurbishment work. However, this had not been finished as the couple had fallen out so precipitating the sale. But it did have a good-sized kitchen-dining room with French doors to the garden which was one of the features on our wish list.

Marilyn however could see more in it than me. She thought the private cul-de-sac of only a few nice houses had something special about it and I couldn't argue on that score. She could see through the scruffy condition of the interior and particularly loved the garden and had a vision of how beautiful it could be from the outset. Her view was that location was the all-important thing whereas the condition could be improved. "*Worst house – best road.*" was her maxim. The more I looked and thought about it I could certainly see her point but it didn't make me like it any more. But I did know it was important to get all of our cash back into property as soon as possible and went along with her although to my mind it was more as a 'do up and move on' project than our forever home.

Our offer on Coltsfoot was accepted on Valentine's Day 2000 and the sale completed in April. Entering the property after receiving the keys we looked around and were close to tears.

We knew the house needed some work but once clear of furniture with empty rooms and bare walls it just looked so awful. It's amazing how little you notice on a house viewing and now without the furniture, all the defects were laid out in full view. Where cupboards and chimney breasts had been removed the ceilings and walls had not been made good; it needed total redecoration which we had anticipated but somehow the worse thing was that the previous owners who kept chickens had obviously let them roam the house and their droppings were all over the floors. We said, *"What on earth have we done?"*

Just at this point, Marilyn happened to look out of the window only to see a friend's car creeping slowly by. *"Oh no!"* she said. *"It's Jenny and Doug."* Friends were the last people we wanted to see at that moment but we dried our eyes, put on our brave faces and went outside. They hadn't actually come to call but were just doing a 'drive-by' out of curiosity and I think were embarrassed to have been spotted. So, with all our false faces on we said our cheery hello's and brought them inside. They made a lot of positive and encouraging sounds but we all knew it was not a pretty picture.

We'd had a survey done and knew the house was fundamentally sound but it was just the shock in the first moment that got to us. There was a lot of work ahead. As his son didn't need the property until later in the year our buyer agreed we could stay on in the Shalford flat as his tenants for a couple of months while we did the necessary work. It also turned out that he had a kitchen supply business and he agreed that his chief designer could come and advise on refitting the kitchen that was our main priority. In the event, we bought the kitchen from him fairly close to a trade price. Talk about falling on our feet.

I started work on the house immediately after completion and was busy knocking out a former kitchen larder wall when a neighbour called. Introducing himself as Ken Price he asked if we were alright for milk and tea etc. and if I had whatever tools I needed. How charming, and it just got better from there on as we met other neighbours and started to find our way around the friendly village that is Peaslake.

We had other work to arrange too and fortunately had the funds to put things in hand. As well as a new kitchen and complete redecoration the jobs included some wiring upgrades, a new bathroom and work on the central heating. New windows were also going to be needed to replace the old metal-framed ones and some work to redesign the front access to provide space for both our cars so all in all, it was quite a big job.

To make a long story short, we eventually moved into Coltsfoot in June 2000 and with all rooms furnished we still had a garage full of stuff including some furniture and numerous unpacked boxes that had come out of store and that we had not seen since before we went to Spain.

In Fittleworth I'd had the luxury of a beautiful big garage/workshop but now my workbench, tools and all the 'useful' stuff a man keeps were jammed into one end of the garage with a wonky door and ivy growing through the eaves and down the inside walls like the hanging gardens. It took us several months but eventually, everything was unpacked and either brought in again or 'rationalised' via local charity shops or the bin men. This left me with more space as the garage was actually a double-length structure and with the door fixed and shelving installed, I soon had my workshop setup organized once again. A bit cramped for space but ready to do stuff and with enough space at the front end for one car.

The garden needed loads of work including a lot of clearing in the process of which we discovered an old air-raid shelter obscured beneath a huge mound of brambles. We toyed with the idea of keeping it as a kind of garden store but it wasn't really right so decided to demolish it. This proved a great deal easier said than done as it was steel-reinforced concrete so once again, we enlisted some muscle in the shape of Marilyn's nephew Geoff and a big sledgehammer to which it eventually succumbed.

The former chicken run was well manured when the hens weren't busy crapping in the house so we dug it over and planned to have the area as a veg plot.

Some effort had been made to manage the chicken manure via a plastic in-ground composter but it had been strangely placed in the middle of the lawn. I dug it out, dumped the remaining revolting contents into the hole and refilled it with soil. A short time later we had to move a small pear sapling that was in the wrong position so I decided to plant it where the composter had been. Honestly, you could almost see it grow. It went off like a rocket and was proof positive that chicken shit is an excellent fertilizer.

Close to the house, there was a full-width terrace that we initially thought was grass until we discovered that it was just overgrown concrete slabs so that too had to be cleared as well as a couple of small pine trees that were growing up through it. All of the beds were overgrown and needed completely clearing, digging and replanting which we got stuck into with enthusiasm, reshaping some beds in the process.

Overgrown state of the back garden at Coltsfoot.

It took some months to get the garden tidy and that was without any actual redesigning. This however would have to wait a bit as part of the project would be a new stone-paved terrace which would be expensive and was not immediately urgent.

Our redesigned garden

How we eventually transformed Coltsfoot

ii

Once I'd re-opened my workshop so to speak it rekindled my enthusiasm for some hands-on woodworking so I got back in touch with Jenny and Mike the antique dealers at Horsham I'd worked for previously. I told them I was back in the country and said I was available to work with them again if they wanted me to. They said there would certainly be some work but that it might be more about ferrying stock about in their van than actual restoration work. I didn't mind what I did so long as I felt occupied and useful and it brought a few pounds in so that was fine.

It was probably a bit soon but with my mind on trying to earn a bit more to top up the police pension I decided to try and get the handyman thing going again that had done me so well down in Fittleworth so I put an advert in the parish magazine. I called the business "Ask Brian Handyman Services". Almost immediately I started to get some enquiries but was only really able to take on smallish jobs as my workshop space was still a bit limited but more importantly, I was already working two or three days a week for the antique dealers.

With the initial and more urgent jobs done in the house and garden, we had a little more time to spare and decided to respond to an invitation from a Danish couple we had met in Spain to visit them in Copenhagen.

We had never been there before so it was a fun and interesting few days, especially knowing a couple of locals who were kind enough to put us up and show us around some of the main places of interest.

One wet afternoon after visiting 'The Little Mermaid' we were by ourselves in the port area sitting out a shower in a café and reminiscing about our Spanish adventure and realised that we both still had a bit of a hankering after the idea of some sort of accommodation business. Marilyn was by this time also doing a few casual hours at the Guildford Tourist Office so knew there was a need in the area and said *"We could always convert the garage for bed and breakfast I suppose"*

I didn't think it was a runner because the garage was quite narrow. However, we sketched out a sort of plan on a serviette that could potentially provide a smallish but adequate double bedroom to the front, a shower room in the centre and a sitting and breakfast room in the back overlooking the garden. Subject to actual measurements confirming our ideas we thought it could be a real possibility although we had to find out a bit more from the tourism authorities and check out some planning issues.

When we got back it didn't take long to confirm that the measurements would just about work so we started to make some enquiries about minimum requirements and discovered The Pink Book which is a guide the tourist authority provided to accommodation suppliers who want to be graded and listed in the authority's guide book and web pages. And that in short is how The Garden Room B&B was born although of course, it didn't come into being that fast, mainly because the garage was still occupied by one car and my make-do workshop. So the first thing on the agenda was to relocate my workspace.

I'd already built one garage/workshop and of course could easily have done another but as time was something of an issue now, we decided to buy one in and locate it in the garden where the chickens had been and the embryonic veg patch was about to be laid out.

It was a decent area and so once again I was away with the fairies in my mind as to what sort of super-duper workspace I could create. I envisaged a wonderful 'man cave' (if only I could get away with it !!) We also wanted it to be something attractive rather than one of the rectangular boxes on offer from most of the garden building suppliers. After a few enquiries, we found a company that was a bit more flexible and used a CAD system for designing their buildings.

So, when we said we'd like a little sitting-out area it was a matter of moments on a computer to input the dimensions of the old chicken run and suddenly, on the screen was the perfect L shaped garden building with the cutest little deck that we immediately christened "Gin and Tonic Corner". We were really getting into this.

At about six by six metres, it was certainly a worthwhile building and although I wasn't planning to build it, I had a lot of ideas about the way I wanted it set up and finished to provide my dream workshop. This was the part I decided to undertake myself.

I knew water and power would be needed so that was the first job that involved laying a twenty-two-metre water supply and mains cable from the back of the existing garage.

I also knew that there would be several machines along with light and heating to be installed so a fuse board and ring mains were also needed all of which I did myself although strictly speaking I probably shouldn't have done as I am not a formally qualified electrician. Full insulation, lining and decoration completed the job and before too long it was possible to transfer all my kit from the cramped area at the back of the garage to this wonderful new space.

My new workshop plus the 'gin and tonic' deck

The inside of my new workshop pictured a few months down the line.

The perfect 'man-cave'

9 THE GARDEN ROOM

i

I was conscious of the need to make a start on the garage conversion but access to my tools and good working space were also going to be important requirements so I had determined that the workshop and machinery would be set up and available before I started on the new B&B space. So it was well into 2001 before I finished the workshop and had it arranged to my satisfaction.

We had contacted the planning office who created no obstacles as we were only going to be changing the use of an existing building although, to be honest, we did only describe it as a guest annexe rather than a prospective accommodation business.

This was partly true as Marilyn had an elderly uncle who enjoyed visiting us and for whom the new ground floor accessible accommodation was ideally suited. Sadly, he didn't live long enough to visit many times although other friends did.

We were fortunate with the design of the garage building as, unusually for an outbuilding, it had cavity walls so no additional wall insulation was needed. Trevor our bricklayer friend who had worked for us before came along and removed the garage door and bricked it up and we arranged for new window units to be installed at the same time. So far so good. Now the interior was all down to me. Although it was a big job it wasn't so very daunting but I knew it would take a while.

Here I think is the moment to skip ahead somewhat because although I could happily go on at length about the job it's not for everyone. Sufficient to say the layout we had envisaged worked out very well and after several months work building stud walls, laying floors, installing insulation, plumbing, wiring etc. I felt we were doing quite well. However, not well enough for Marilyn it seemed, who was impatient to get the business underway so, to spur me on in the final furlong, she took a booking. This really was going to be tight and so to finish the job we had to get help with tiling the shower room which was unfortunate as I had rather wanted to do it myself.

Now I am fine with having ideas and seeing how they might be brought to fruition as well as the practical execution. However, I freely admit I'm not a finisher, much preferring to move on in my head to the next project than dotting and crossing the final i's and t's. Marilyn on the other hand is very much a detail person and it was without any doubt her attention to the small details of the decoration, furnishing and equipment of the rooms that made the business the success it eventually turned out to be. That is, however jumping ahead somewhat because at that time we had no idea how things would pan out.

The bedroom we created as part of our B&B operation.

ii

The set-up we operated for our B&B was driven by the fact that we had no suitable accommodation in the house for either paying guests to sleep or for feeding them and to be honest that is not the way we wanted to do it as we value our privacy.

The Garden Room, named for its attractive garden view; was set up in a self-contained and more or less self-catering arrangement. Furnished with both a breakfast bar and stools overlooking the garden and with seats at a table, the breakfast-sitting room was equipped initially with TV, all crockery and cutlery, kettle, toaster and fridge into which we placed the makings of a pretty comprehensive continental breakfast. This also included the offer of warm croissants and freshly brewed coffee brought out at a time of our guests' choosing.

Initially, we didn't have a clue how this would work. Clearly, there was no cooked breakfast on offer nor a high level of personal service apart from a friendly welcome and offer of any helpful information. However, in practice, it worked very well indeed. Guests appeared to enjoy the arrangement and, in many cases, said that they preferred the privacy of the self-catering set-up and the fact that they did not need to get dressed to appear in a dining room at any fixed time.

We made a point of being very welcoming with the offer of refreshment on arrival and in practice soon found we could identify those guests who were happy to be more sociable and those who liked to be a little reserved. The Garden Room worked very well for both temperaments.

We also had no idea what type of clients our accommodation would attract and were surprised how often we had business people visiting the area for two or three days. The advantage they told us was that in addition to being cheaper than a hotel the two-room layout enabled them to relax and work without having to sit on a hotel bed with a laptop on their knees. They also liked the rural location and the village pub for an evening meal.

One of our early guests was called Brian and was initially booked for a fortnight while he worked on a job in Guildford. He eventually stayed with us for ten months as the job grew and so did his booking. He went home on Fridays so we could still accept weekend bookings which was an ideal arrangement.

Brian was in many ways the perfect guest. A former submariner, he was very tidy and accustomed to living in small spaces and on some days when we went into the annexe it was hard to tell if he had been there or not.

One day when we went to service the room, we found a tray of meat marinating in the fridge and when Brian came home from work with a bottle of Sancerre under his arm he said *"Ok. Get the barbi out I'm cooking tonight."*

We had several long-term guests like Brian. Laura was from Swindon but working in Guildford and was with us more than eighteen months and has become a very dear friend. We asked one of the longer-term guests if there was anything that would make their stay more convenient. They asked if a microwave would be possible to avoid having to either eat cold or pay for eating out each evening. We willingly provided one and it seemed that the set-up was complete with the ability to heat ready-meals or knock up scrambled eggs and soup.

Over our 15 years as B&B owners we only had one seriously negative experience. This was fairly early on when we had a mother and daughter as guests for a couple of nights. They were apparently in the process of moving house and couldn't get into their new home for a couple of days. They were charming in all respects but when they left, we found they had helped themselves to all the towels and all the toiletries along with a couple of books and the entire contents of the fridge including containers plus one or two other things that I can't now remember. Being our first such experience it did come as a bit of a shock.

During those years at Peaslake, we met so many really lovely people, many of whom have returned on several occasions and have become friends. It was a great idea and apart from earning us quite a lot of money over the years has been an important and enjoyable part of our lives.

10 PEASLAKE

i

The first couple of years at Peaslake appeared to fly by and in no-time we felt like we'd been there forever. The road we had chosen, or perhaps I should say, Marilyn had chosen; was perfect in so many ways. While Limbourne Lane in Fittleworth had been a nice place to live, the majority of residents there were older than us and mostly retired people of some means so in retrospect it's true to say that we never felt totally comfortable there.

Let's be honest we were a couple of council house kids who had done alright and the locals were pleasant and polite if not exactly warm towards us (with the notable exception of Mike and Jill and Tom and Yvonne who lived next door.) So, while we felt Ok, we were conscious that in some way we didn't quite fit.

This was born out on one occasion when we were invited to 'pre-dinner drinks' at a neighbour's house. Not being that accustomed to such gatherings, we assumed this was going to be an evening out with drinks and dinner to follow so we had nothing to eat and headed off to the neighbour's and tucked into some tasty canapés and large glasses of wine.

What we couldn't quite understand was why there didn't appear to be any dinner preparation going on and it was only when other neighbours began to say their *thank-you's* and started to leave that it dawned on us that *pre-dinner* drinks meant drinks before returning to dinner at your own place. Ah! Well you live and learn.

Crest Hill Peaslake on the other hand, was very much our kind of street. There was no-one who could have been said to be snobbish or superior. They were almost entirely what I would call ordinary working people across the range from bankers and brokers to builders, technicians to teachers and shop assistants plus a couple of retirees. Friendly and salt of the earth pretty much without exception. I mentioned Ken Price and his offer of tools and tea when I was working in the house and he was no exception. There was a great sense of community in the street that included a communal barbecue that could be used by anyone for their own private events although it was not unusual for the current holder of the BBQ to do a ring round and say *"The BBQ's going. Want to bring something round?"* Arriving with your bottle and burgers it was quite likely that half the street was already in attendance.

Another example of the community in action was concerning road maintenance. Our short cul-de-sac was unadopted by the council so we were liable for the maintenance. There was a road committee of two or three who monitored the condition of the gravel surface and the depth and number of any pot-holes and when deemed necessary a date was set for communal road mending. A lorry load of gravel and scalpings was ordered and a JCB borrowed from a friendly local farmer for the price of a bottle or two. And on the agreed date everyone turned out with picks, rakes and shovels and set to repairing the holes and spreading a new gravel surface and the price was rarely more than £35 to £40 a house every two or three years.

The working party was kept liberally supplied with beer or coffee and cakes from various kitchens and all in all it was a great community bonding event. Most summers one of us would put on a drinks gathering in or outdoors depending on the weather and likewise at Christmas and in 2002 we had a street party to celebrate the Queen's Golden Jubilee. We didn't live in each other's pockets as in a Coronation Street stereotype but such was the community in our little road that you felt that in an emergency you could knock on any door and get help.

ii

The wider community in Peaslake took a little longer to infiltrate, not in any sense because we were kept out but simply because whilst we quickly became on nodding terms with folk we saw around the place and the staff in the village shop you don't become 'friends' based on casual encounters or at least we didn't.

The trick it seems is to become a 'joiner'. There was a local 'wives' group and although this was not exactly Marilyn's type of thing she joined up as a way to get to know a few people. It worked very well and almost as soon as she joined, we found ourselves in fancy dress wandering the streets with cutlery and glass as part of a 'travelling party' moving from one host's home to another. A great way to get acquainted and break down a few barriers. A bit later she also joined the bell-ringers at Shere which opened a door to a whole new social circle of interesting and varied characters.

For my part, I offered up my practical skills to help build scenery for the local amateur dramatic groups and here Marilyn also became involved in doing front-of-house duties and serving interval refreshment. So, one way and another by the time we had been in the village two or three years we were pretty well involved and really loving our lives there.

Dog ownership is another great way to get chatting with people. As mentioned earlier we had lost our dear little Benjy just before setting off for Spain the previous year and he was sadly missed. We had however decided to leave it a while and try to go without for a period because whatever you say, dogs are a bit of a tie and we wanted the freedom to come and go easily as we pleased.

This was hard and it wasn't long before our resolve crumbled and we decided to get another. We have always had rescue dogs and so we got in touch with a local organization that put us in touch with a local dog re-homing group. They in turn told us about a dog owned by a young single mum living in a rented farm cottage who had a dog that needed to be re-homed so we went and met Robbie.

A real mongrel, Robbie was a Lurcher – Bearded Collie – Border Collie cross which was effectively a four-way mix although the Beardie characteristics were the strongest. He had to be tied up most of the time because the owner couldn't afford to fence the garden and Robbie who was super friendly was in the habit of going 'walkies' with anyone who passed or giving chase to passing vehicles.

Walking him a couple of times a day around the village or the local Hurtwood forest we soon found ourselves getting to know other dog owners and it was really interesting how quickly we and Robbie became part of the local scene.

By this time, we were leading quite busy lives for a couple of retirees and between us were running a couple of businesses, namely The Garden Room bed and breakfast venture which was doing far better than we had dared to expect and my woodworking handyman activities including work for the antique dealers.

iii

Unusually, I think it was me that one day noticed an advert in the local paper for a part-time casual role with the Guildford office of Savills the estate agents. The job was to join a team of 'house viewing assistants' who would be available on an ad hoc basis to come along at short notice to accompany potential buyers to view properties. I was interested in building construction and design; felt I would be comfortable getting back into a semi-sales role; (Here I'm harking back to my time flogging cars in the '60s.); it would introduce another albeit probably small income stream but I think most of all because it appealed to my nosiness. After all, Savills are very top-end in the property market and the idea of wandering around multi-million-pound mansions was quite exciting.

So I applied and got the job where I found I was the only male among a group of ladies who like me were attracted by the idea of nosing around other people's houses. They were quite a 'county' bunch if you know what I mean. Ladies of a certain age and station, and when it came to the occasional group meeting or briefing, I can't say I felt exactly one of the team. However, I did enjoy the work and made a huge effort to acquaint myself with individual properties. Also, I always made a point of being on-site well in advance of the viewing client to find my way around the houses and anticipate any likely questions about the property or local environs.

I enjoyed the job so much in fact that I asked Tommy de Mallet-Morgan, the then head of office at Guildford if there was any way in which I could become more involved. He must have liked what I was doing and came up with an interesting offer. His idea was that I should take responsibility for the pre-marketing activity. This meant that once a pitch to a potential vendor had been made and instructions received it would be my job to arrange for floor plans and photographs to be done and then to go along to the property and prepare the particulars, in other words, the sales brochure text. As I loved writing and coupled with the opportunity to visit even more interesting houses, this was right up my street.

From time to time, I do wonder why, apart from my obvious charm and intellect (being ironic here), I have managed to walk into jobs like this so easily and have concluded that it is quite likely to be the ex-police effect.

Hopefully with good reason, it seems that people still do have a level of confidence in the 'police' label and see us as being honest and trustworthy enough to allow into their lives or employment in the ways I've described. It was certainly the case with the handyman role I performed for many years and later with other work including with Savills.

Both aspects of the job were interesting in different ways. As a viewing assistant, I met a wide range of potential buyers most of whom were lovely; polite and normal or as normal as a person thinking of spending several million pounds could be to me. A few, and it was often the 'new money' individuals, were harder going.

Bearing in mind my relatively humble origins I did have a job getting my head around the amount of money involved and the casual way such huge expenditure was apparently viewed.

By way of conversation and to provide some feedback to the office I would sometimes ask about the sale of an existing property and was surprised how often folks from London would be down in the Surrey Hills looking to spend a couple of million or more on a weekend hideaway with no plans to sell their existing homes. Given my own more or less 'shoestring' house purchase history this was right outside my experience or comprehension. I remember one day showing a woman and her friend around a £3,000,000 country house with acres of land and hearing her say to her friend *"It's lovely. Do you know what, I might just buy it and tell John later."* Presumably, John was her husband. I could hardly believe my ears.

The other element, which was more or less a copywriting role was different again. Basically, for a sales brochure I had four sections to fill:

- directions to the property via the most attractive route if there was a choice,
- the situation of the property relative to the rest of the area including communications by road and rail, local amenities, schools and recreational opportunities,
- description of the property itself
- and the gardens and grounds.

I loved meeting the vendors and getting to understand what they thought the key features and selling points of their homes were so that I could maximize them in my text. It was also fascinating to learn about the history of some of the houses, many of which were period buildings with really interesting backgrounds including famous former owners or being significant elements in important events. To give a context to a property I would often spend hours in on-line research, far more than I ever felt able to claim on my timesheets. I just enjoyed doing it.

iv

I did have one other little business idea in those first few years at Peaslake which arose directly from my handyman activities for local families. I noticed on a couple of occasions that whilst I was working for someone, holiday plans were being hatched and on another occasion, the family SUV was being loaded up for the trip to the airport.

It occurred to me that I might be able to offer a service of driving people to the airports in their own cars. The cars could then be returned to their garages so saving a quite significant airport parking fee and providing confidence that their vehicles were safely tucked up at home. I could then pick up the vehicle again to meet their return flights. There is nothing worse than arriving off a long flight and then having to drag luggage onto a bus to the long-term car park. I certainly seemed to hit the spot with this idea too because the family I first mentioned it to almost literally jumped at the offer. Although I charged a bit less than our local airport taxis it was not so much the cost issue that attracted people because most of my clients in and around that area had more than enough money. I think it was more the convenience and appeal of being met by a face they knew and in a familiar vehicle too.

The first family that I did this for told their friends and before long I was on the car insurance of several local families and not only for airport trips. Chauffeuring for social events came into my brief and even ferrying their offspring to and from their boarding schools on occasion. The process worked in reverse too because once people got to know me as a driver, I naturally told them about my other activities and so started to pick up more of the handyman jobs as a result.

If all this sounds as if we were both working our socks off that wasn't exactly the case although we did have as much work as we needed around that time. The real beauty of the situations was firstly the variety which as they say is *'the spice of life'* and the fact that we could pretty much pick and choose how much or little we wanted to do and what could be better than that?

11   MORE ABOUT SPAIN

i

Given all I've said about our liking for Spain, you won't be surprised to learn there is more to come.

In 2002, Lucea, one of the Spanish girls we had arranged accommodation for when we were in Fittleworth, contacted us to ask whether her boyfriend Pablo might be able to come and stay with us. He wanted to improve his English and he hoped he might be able to find work in the area for the month or so he planned to stay. We were very happy to oblige but pointed out that we were some distance out of Guildford with relatively poor public transport links but if he was happy to come on that basis, he'd be very welcome. We also said that in the meantime we would try to find him some work nearby to avoid him having to go into town. As luck would have it, we did manage to find him a post working in the White Horse pub in Shere.

Pablo was a lovely boy who was at that time still at university studying English in La Coruña which for those who don't know is in Galicia in the far north-west of Spain. We liked him immediately and in the same way we had with Alex years before, we took him unreservedly into the family. This included taking him out on trips to local places of interest and doing as much as we could to help him develop his confidence in the English language. In his school and university, he had received a very good grounding in English as far as grammar and vocabulary were concerned but his tutors were almost exclusively Spanish so he had hardly ever heard the language spoken without an accent. His work at the pub went a long way to helping in that respect but it was a very steep learning curve.

Poor Pablo didn't know whether he was coming or going. He had never worked before in his twenty years so finding himself as a waiter in the hurly-burly of a busy English country pub left him mentally and physically exhausted. I must confess we did laugh as we listened to him on the phone to his father saying how hard it was and how tired he was and especially when he explained his father's reaction was along the lines of "*Welcome to the real world son.*"

Pablo wanted to teach but the difficulty was that he couldn't hope for a post in the public sector in Spain without an additional examination. Known as '*Oposiciones*' this further hurdle is notoriously difficult to jump and thousands of young people find their careers stalled for years while they try, often on multiple occasion, to pass the exam. Public sector employment has always been the most secure employment in Spain and has historically more or less guaranteed a job for life so naturally is a very common aspiration. Frankly, this extra exam layer seems to be mainly in place to simply ration the opportunities for these sought-after posts.

Understandably, Pablo's parents were anxious for his long-term job security and therefore encouraged him to pursue this course but Pablo wanted to move his life on. An alternative would have been to go for a teaching post in the private sector but here teaching experience was a requirement which he did not have.

It occurred to us that he could perhaps try another route and told him how I had been offered immediate teaching posts after the English Teaching course I did in Guildford a few years before. We suggested to him that he could do the same course as me to obtain his teaching qualification and then seek experience outside of Spain, even temporarily.

His parents weren't keen and I don't think we were exactly flavour of the month when he decided to do just that. The following year he came back and worked for a couple of weeks in the pub again to get his ear in and then went every day to classes in Guildford. Each evening I helped him with his lesson preparation and then we both acted as his stooge students as he gave his practice lessons in our sitting room at home.

He put in a huge effort and was rewarded with his own TEFL diploma (Now known as ESL – English as Second Language.)

At this time, he still had a year or two to go with his university course but at least he had the English teaching qualification.

ii

It was hardly surprising that with all this connection being maintained, our love and interest in Spain was undiminished. Quite the contrary in fact, so that in 2004 our thoughts turned again to how we might deepen our connection with the country. We had rather lost our nerve with our previous experience but decided that perhaps a small holiday property out there might fit the bill and started looking for flats and once again in Catalunya as this was still the area where we had the most contacts.

The actual purchase when it came happened quite quickly. We had identified a small two-bed apartment in the coastal town of Roses at the northern end of the Costa Brava not very far from the French border and arranged a trip out together to have a look at it. In the event, the property was sold the day we arrived and unfortunately there was nothing similar that we were taken with. But then the agent told us of another that was just about to be offered in Empuriabrava and although it had just one bedroom, we felt we might as well have a look.

We both thought it was ideal. Smaller than we had originally intended but perfectly adequate given that it would usually be just the two of us there. The price and location were right so we agreed to buy it and saved ourselves a few Euros too as it was cheaper than the one we had originally gone out to see.

Given that our idea the first time we decided to move to Spain was to stay off the tourist trail and plant ourselves in the heart of the countryside, this was a surprising purchase because Empuriabrava is a coastal resort and about as un-Spanish as you can imagine. However, as a small holiday bolt-hole it did (and still does) tick all the boxes.

Following photos give an impression of our little 'home away from home'.

It is unashamedly a tourist resort although less popular with Brits than it is with French and German visitors. It is the largest residential marina in Europe (some say the world) with around twenty-four kilometres of navigable canals and some five thousand. private moorings.

It is also one of the top three sky-diving centres in the world. As a result, it has become the playground of a lot of extremely wealthy people and their (in some cases) ludicrously expensive gin palace boats and luxury cars. There are of course hundreds of less well-off people like us who thoroughly enjoy this pseudo millionaire lifestyle on a shoe string minus boat, huge villas, posh cars or any of the other trappings that can be seen on a stroll around the corner.

We are located just off the main thoroughfare so it is quiet yet within a few metres of our bank, supermarket, and all the bars and restaurants you could wish for. Just 300 metres away the fabulous beach is over a kilometre in length and up to 150 metres deep from the water's edge to the well-maintained promenade with its relatively few and understated bars and discos. Empuriabrava was created in the 1960s from an area of reclaimed swamp and is still bounded on both sides by protected Natural Park that provides superb habitat for a wide range of wild life and also limits further development.

As we are not enthusiastic beach people, more often than not we tend to head away from the coast to the old town of Castello d'Empuries which is our historic and local administrative centre. Here we enjoy the maze of narrow streets, shady squares and shops as well as the impressive basilica of Santa Maria.

Every September there is a medieval fair with a great party atmosphere, artisan market and various entertainments that we usually try to attend.

A little further inland is the larger town of Figueres. This is a very typical Catalan working town well known for its famous son, surrealist artist Salvador Dali, whose fabulous museum is worth a visit. Beyond that and a little further inland one is away from the coastal tourist fringe and as Spanish as you could want with miles of stunning countryside against the wonderful mountain backdrop of the Pyrenees.

During our many previous visits to Catalunya before '99 when looking for potential homes to buy we had become quite familiar with this hinterland but mostly the road network and towns and villages we drove through on the way to somewhere else. Now however, as semi-residents with the flat, we had a little more time to explore and one of our favourite places became the beautiful lake at Banyoles, a medium-sized town about half an hour west of Figueres.

The lake is approximately 2 kilometres long by 750 m with an average depth of 15 m that in several points gets down to almost 50 metres. It is located in a natural tectonic depression and fed by springs. Originating in the nearby volcanic Garrotxa region the waters are slightly warm so swimming is possible in the lake all year round. As a consequence, it has become quite a centre for water sports including rowing and was used for training by the British Olympic team among others. We have developed a little routine around Banyoles that begins with coffee in one of several lakeside cafes followed by an easy flat five-mile walk around the edge and then lunch back at the café. Retirement is tough but someone has to do it.

A bit to the north and west of Banyoles and centred on the town of Olot, the aforementioned Garrotxa area is a protected natural park in the higher foothills of the Pyrenees.

It is easily identifiable as volcanic in origin by the classic conical shape of the hills in the area. The region is also well known for its rather high annual rainfall and is referred to by locals as *"l'orinal de Catalunya"* (the urinal of Catalunya). Together with the rich volcanic soil, this has given rise to extensive areas of dense forest that cover the region.

One area particularly worth a visit is the *Fageda d'en Jordá,* a tranquil and beautiful beech forest on ancient lava where paths meander beneath a shady canopy around and between huge mounds of dark aerated pumice stone.

These would originally have been 'lava bombs' meaning that these huge chunks of red-hot stone would at some time long past have come raining out of the sky which is a truly terrifying thought.

Unsurprisingly I guess, we were like kids with a new toy around the flat and either together or separately in those first few months we were back and forth to Empuriabrava as often as we could. There were things we wanted to do to improve the place as nothing had been done since it was originally built in the 1970s. These included total redecoration, a new kitchen and a shower room upgrade. These all had to be researched and organized so there was a fair bit to do.

In May 2005 I went out with my sister Angela and enjoyed showing her around the area and a bit further afield in Catalunya too and then again Marilyn and I went out together in June. It was lovely to catch up again with Alex's family in Barcelona and we spent a really fun time with them and their friends on the fiesta of San Juan when they threw a great party at their home. We have been many times since and it is always huge fun.

By this time our Spanish was becoming quite reasonable and curiously the more wine we drank the better it became. Well, that was how it seemed to me although others might not agree. Truth is though that whilst certainly far from perfect we were more than able to carry on a conversation which is what matters when all is said and done.

Our friendship with Pablo and his family continued and in July 2005 he came to visit us in Peaslake with his mother Cristina. Sadly, his father was unable to get away at the time. We very much enjoyed the opportunity to get to know Cristina better and as we had done with her son the previous year, we played our tour guide roles and made sure she saw as much of Surrey and the south coast as she could in the time we had together.

iii

Our enthusiasm for Spain was such at this time that we decided a longer visit was needed but what to do about the B&B. Fortunately, my sister had a friend who spent a lot of time house sitting and pet caring. To our great delight she was even up for running the B&B too so in September 2005 we were off again to the flat leaving the lovely Lynne in charge of all in our absence.

The idea was to meander slowly west from the flat along the foot of the Pyrenees exploring anywhere that looked interesting before turning along the north coast to catch up again with Pablo and his family in La Coruña.

We had planned to find a night's accommodation in the Cerdanya, an easy few hour's drive from the coast. This beautiful area is a hidden high-level valley in the heart of the Pyrenees and is popular with walkers, cyclists and nature lovers as it enjoys an alpine climate and a high level of sunshine throughout the year.

Unfortunately for us, something we ate in the evening meal at our overnight stop seriously disagreed with us and we felt so bad the following day that any notion of a relaxed meander over a few days went totally by the board. We decided to head as quickly as we could to the north coast city of San Sebastian where we sought out a medical centre for some advice. Fairly predictably I guess the advice was *"Take it easy for a couple of days and drink plenty."* which is exactly what Marilyn had been saying anyway. So, after a couple of days of R&R in beautiful San Sebastian, we set off again towards the west and more or less following the north coast.

By-passing the major centres of Bilbao and Santander we had decided to head for the Picos de Europa National Park in the rugged Cantabrian Mountains that in this area span the border between the regions of Cantabria and Asturias. Commonly known as *'España Verde'* or 'Green Spain' on account of the high rainfall and lush grass; this is another region that whilst not overly well-known worldwide is nevertheless a magnet for walkers, off-road bikers, nature lovers and in this region climbers too.

From the north coast, access to the Picos National Park is via a very narrow and tortuous road that for a large part of its route is cut into a ledge in the near-vertical side of a narrow gorge known as the *Desfiladero de la hermida* – 'the hermit's gorge'. It is certainly a bit hair-raising as the road in places is extremely tight with vertical drops to the tumbling mountain-blue water of the river Deva far below.

We stayed for a night in the pretty and rustic town of Potes although the B&B we found was less than perfect as the owners' kids were a couple of unruly, and we thought rude, nine or ten-year-olds who were simply allowed to run riot around the guests. Not fun. The food was OK but the beds nothing special so all in all the following morning we were pleased to move on and further into the Picos mountains. Access to the main range, and recommended for a spectacular high-level walk, was via a cable car station at Fuente Dé.

There is no village here, just the cable car *(teleferico)*, although there is a Parador hotel and a couple of bars as I recall. Installed in the sixties the cable car is an impressive system with the longest unsupported single-span lift in Europe and it carries the twenty-person cabins up almost 2500 feet in a little under five minutes and rewards with most amazing distant views although looking down is a bit tummy churning. The cabin starts its ascent at what seems a relatively normal angle but by about two-thirds of the way up it is much nearer to the face of the mountain and seems to arrive close to vertically and almost through the floor of the upper station.

Stepping out from the cabin and looking around, the view is breathtaking because at that level the Picos consist of bare, near-white limestone that almost dazzles in the sunlight. There are several walks of varying duration from the upper station including the longest of some nine km back down to the Parador. We went for a relatively short walk towards what in the distance looked like a very small mountain cabin with a red roof. As we drew closer it became obvious that it was more substantial; in fact it was more of a mansion that we later learnt was a former royal hunting lodge.

Heading back out of the Picos and towards Potes we passed through the achingly pretty village of Espinama where to Marilyn's horror we were brought to a stop by a herd of very long-horned cattle being driven along the road some of whom would have had their heads in the window had she not been pretty damn quick to close it. It was a difficult route to drive because the stunning views almost obliged one to stop and snatch a photo as each successive vista opened up.

The Picos from Espinama

Taking a left (west) along the main coast road brought us to the town of Cangas de Onis and the nearby sanctuary of Covadonga.

Cangas lies to the northwest of the Picos de Europa. For fifty years following the battle of Covadonga in 772 AD, it was the capital of the kingdom of Asturias, and therefore of Christian Spain. A Roman bridge crosses the River Sella on the edge of town, and nearby is the 8th century chapel of Santa Cruz constructed around an even older dolmen. Cangas de Onís has a variety of shops, bars, restaurants, and hotels, and holds a busy Sunday market.

Twelve km south-east of Cangas de Onís, Covadonga is the historic site of the battle that shaped Spain's destiny, and a major pilgrimage destination. The cathedral is stunningly situated in a deep green forested valley, next to the sacred cave and waterfall. We tried to drive to the lake and waterfall which are by all accounts very much worth a visit but I bottled out owing to the narrowness of the roads with precipitous drops and the high likelihood of having to back up for one of the many tourist coaches using the route.

Continuing along the north coast we were heading for La Coruña the capital of Galicia, another of Spain's autonomous regions, where we were to meet Pablo along with his parents Juan and Cristina. The coastline in this area is particularly beautiful and known as the *Rias Altas*. Ria is the term for a coastline characterised by long and often multi-branching inlets formed from flooded former river valleys. This differs from the fiord coastline which has glacial origins. I have always loved water in the landscape so here I was in heaven as the ria coastline offered us some of the most beautiful land and seascape views I'd ever seen.

Crystal clear water and long beaches of silver sand were tempting but on dipping a toe we found the Atlantic water very cold. Which explains why coastal tourism is still quite undeveloped in the area and the majority of foreign visitors at least still head for the 'sea, sun and Sangria' of the Mediterranean coast. 'Thank goodness' is my response to that and along with the many Spanish holiday-makers from the hot south and centre and a few others in the know, we have been back to Galicia now more times than we can count.

Having mentioned briefly the significance of Catalan as a separate regional language within Spain it is perhaps worth a mention that Catalunya is not unique in this respect. Apart from what might be described as strong local dialects and accents (as we have in the UK), there are a number of other quite distinct languages of which Galician (*Gallego*) spoken in Galicia is one and *Valenciano* another. Both these are recognisable to the ear as being similar to Castilian Spanish although the differences are still considerable. *Gallego* is more akin to Portuguese which is not surprising given its location just to the north of Portugal. Aranese is another that is spoken alongside Catalan along the eastern Pyrenees but the real stranger in the camp is Basque (*Euskera*).

It is spoken in the western end of the Pyrenees in the area around Bilbao and known as the Basque Country *(Pais Vasco)*. This has a very different sound and the spelling and letter usage are to most outsiders really strange.

iv

It was around mid-September 2005 when we arrived in La Coruña and were royally welcomed by Pablo and his lovely parents Juan and Cristina, brother Pedro as well as Juan's mother Josefina who lived with them. Their home, in common with so many Spanish people is a spacious city apartment but this one was on the 4th floor with no lift so was not unchallenging for us, unaccustomed as we were to serious stair climbing. We were mega impressed by *la abuela* (grandmother) who at around eighty years of age climbed the stairs at least twice daily to venture into town for her regular walk and meetings for coffee with friends.

Now, in the same way that we had taken Pablo and Cristina around our home area, Juan had planned a quite comprehensive tour of north-west Galicia for our education. On the first day, he introduced us to the gruesomely named Coast of Death *(Costa da Morte* in Gallego*)*. This is the majority of the north-west corner of Galicia and so named for the number of shipwrecks over the centuries along its treacherous and rocky shore.

Even quite recently and with the benefit of modern navigational aids this dangerously exposed coast continues to claim victims – notably the tanker MV Prestige which foundered there in 2002 spilling thousands of tons of heavy oil. The clean-up was still going on when we visited and the environmental damage was catastrophic. On a more cheerful note, this same coast is also known as the shellfish coast *(Costa do Marisco)* where its numerous pretty fishing villages are the source of some of the most superb shellfish, much of which is exported to high-class restaurants world-wide.

Cape Finisterra was also very well worth a visit to see the rather impressive lighthouse and stand on the cliffs looking westward and contemplate the 3400 km of Atlantic between there and the next landfall at St Johns Newfoundland. It tended to put things in perspective. Finisterra is also popular with pilgrims who, having walked the route to Santiago de Compostela, sometimes feel compelled to continue to the coast.
Here traditionally they burn their boots and rush into the sea naked, presumably to rinse off the dust of many miles travelled. We certainly saw the remains of boots burnt but no naked pilgrims. A bit cold I guess.

Like the northern coast, this is also a ria coastline and is if anything an even better example with no less than four huge estuarine inlets. Being west-facing it is in line for all the moist air from the Atlantic but generally, this is not deposited as rain on the coastal plain but a little further inland where the land starts to rise.

As a result, the actual coast enjoys a pleasant micro-climate that makes it a very attractive place to visit. It may not be that great for bathing as the sea is cooler than the southern coasts but the long white sandy beaches are ideal for sun lovers and the area enjoys a good if not huge tourist industry. The majority of hotels are centred around the main coastal towns and development elsewhere is quite sparse which means woodland and lush green meadows can be found extending right to the water's edge in many places.

This two-mile beach near Ancoradoiro on the west coast of Galicia is typical of those in the area and the more impressive four-mile beach at Carnota.

Las Rias Baixas (Lower Rias) region is a Spanish Denominación de Origen (DO) for wines produced in the province of Pontevedra and the south of the province of Coruña. It is renowned for its white wines made from the Albariño grape variety which are perfectly suited to accompany the local seafood.

Apart from beaches and countryside in this area the architecture is interesting too and is where the longest *horreo* (grain store) is to be found in the village of Carnota. Constructed of local granite and mounted on staddle stones similar to those familiar to us in England; owing to the sometimes extreme weather on this exposed coast the structure is quite closed, having only narrow slots to allow for air circulation.

The horreo at Carnota, at 35 metres in length is the longest in the country.

Juan's excursion for us the next day was inland to the Lugo mountains which are part of the Galician Massif that rise in places to almost 2200 metres. Abundant rainfall on the fertile ground has given rise to a dense cover of temperate deciduous forest where oaks predominate. The woodland alternates with scrubland and wide natural meadows and in the higher spots tree cover gives way to bare moorland topped with rocky outcrops. Here we visited ancient churches, the beautiful monastery at Samos, filled containers with clear fresh spring water at roadside *'fuentes'* and took in some spectacular mountain scenery especially from the vantage point of O Cebreiro. Perched on a ridge at some 1300 m with breathtaking vistas all around, this charming 'hobbit hamlet' welcomes visitors to Galicia as it is on the main pilgrim route to Santiago de Compostela (of which much more later). Too soon our time with this lovely family was over and we were back on the road heading generally in a diagonal line back towards Catalunya but with one more stop to make in Galicia.

v

I mentioned earlier the effects of rural depopulation and indeed Galicia was and still is one of the regions worst affected. With a largely agricultural economy based on individual family holdings or small area co-operatives, living has until quite recently been pretty much at subsistence level. So understandably given the greater access to information nowadays the younger generation is inclined to want a 'slice of the urban action' that staying in the village and taking over from parents is unlikely to provide.

The resulting rural exodus has created a situation in many small villages where the very existence of the villages as viable entities has been jeopardized and this is still very much the situation today. One such village is Cristosende and it was here that our basket-maker friend Lluis and his partner Anna had come to live.

Cristosende in the morning mist.

Surrounded by vine terraces and chestnut woods and perched at some 517m above sea level with views over the deep canyon of the River Sil, the village occupies what to most would seem an idyllic situation. However, notwithstanding its wonderfully picturesque location, at the time we visited we learnt from Anna and Lluis that all was far from well in the village which was more than apparent by the number of abandoned and derelict buildings and the poor state of many of the vine terraces. There were no young children in the village and if I remember correctly Anna and Lluis were the youngest couple living there and Lluis, like me was around 60 years of age.

However, on the positive side, there had been some recent investment in the form of a major refurbishment of the Casa Grande in the village centre. This privately-owned building had been operating as a hotel for some time but the much-needed improvement was made possible via the 'LEADER' scheme. This is a project for the promotion and funding of rural development and intended to overcome some of the many problems such as the depopulation just described. As a result, there was now a trickle of visitors to the village who stayed at the Casa Grande while exploring the beautiful area on foot or bicycle.

The dramatic Sil Canyon. It is this landscape that is beginning to attract more rural tourism in the form of walkers, cyclists and country lovers.

Also, Anna and Lluis's activity as basket-maker and weaver brought a few visitors and so it seemed little by little the area and the village was experiencing a degree of renewal. However, there was a long way to go but since then thanks largely to Anna's use of social media to promote her own and Lluis's craft activity, other craftspeople in the area have begun networking and managed to raise the profile of this little but stunningly beautiful corner of Spain.

At the time of writing, Anna's enterprise has gone from strength to strength as she pushes the boundaries of fabric design which she initially hand weaves before contracting some of the designs out for factory production to meet demand.

Although he still does some teaching, Lluis has to some extent now taken a back seat as far as hands-on basketry is concerned and is mainly involved in running the online shop and website as well as a good half share in the care of young Thomasina. Their enterprise is now so well regarded that university students studying fabric design are admitted as interns to work alongside Anna where they gain an insight into both the design process as well as hands-on weaving and the preparation of the natural vegetable dyes that Anna sources from the local environment. Check out Anna's website at www.annachampeney.com for some stunning fabrics and garments available on-line.

On our most recent visit to Cristosende (September 2019), there was a distinct feeling that a corner has been turned. The hotel is far busier than it was with walkers and cyclists coming in greater numbers. Several of the old derelict houses have been refurbished and four small houses have been built for holiday rental. One just has to hope that this does not go too far or the idyll that so captivated us on our first visit might just be lost.

We left Cristosende and headed more or less diagonally back across country towards the flat in Empuriabrava stopping to overnight along the way at the very ancient and characterful town on Covarrubias and then by-passing Madrid for a second brief stop in Cuenca with its fascinating 'hanging houses' suspended out over the deep gorge that surrounds the town.

Returning to the flat we were pleased to find that the work we had commissioned to take place whilst we were away had indeed been done and we had a lovely newly fitted shower room which was certainly a treat compared to what was there before.

So the end of September 2005 found us back home in Peaslake where we almost seamlessly dropped back into life there and within a couple of weeks it was almost as if we hadn't been away. 'Ask Brian', my handyman enterprise was still getting plenty of enquiries and bringing in a reasonable income as was my work with the antique dealers and the estate agents.

Marilyn was still at the Tourist Office on a part-time basis; the B&B was doing OK and Lynne had presented us with a diary of new future bookings that would take care of the following few months, so all in all we were pretty well and profitably occupied. The problem was that the recent experience had very much rekindled our desire to see more of Spain so in truth, we still had very itchy feet.

12   TIME OUT

i

With Christmas out of the way and a return to what amounted to our version of normality, January 2006 found us still fidgety and starting to think about what our next adventure might be. I think in truth we both knew without saying that it was going to have to be some more of Spain and knowing we had the flat there and ready to occupy at any time we also knew it would be easy to do. We concluded that perhaps we should try once again to go and live there for an extended period that would allow us to get out of holiday mode and get a feel for what 'living' abroad would be like rather than simply visiting.

Clearly, this couldn't just happen at the drop of a hat as we had commitments and B&B bookings to consider. We also knew we couldn't ask Lynne to look after it for such an extended period. In any event, we had decided it would probably be a better financial prospect to rent the house in our absence and use the income to fund our adventure, at least in part.

Implementing such an idea of course also meant that our plans would have to include our dog Robbie. So that meant finding out what was involved in taking a family pet out of and back into the country. Fortunately, by that time the terrible rule requiring months of quarantine had been changed. All that was then required was a 'pet passport', in effect an identity document; rabies vaccination and then a certificate of worming from a vet within 24 hours before arrival back in the UK. Much simpler, so that was no longer an issue.

Once the date was roughly decided we drew a line across the diary for B&B reservations and if I remember correctly, there was only one guest who had booked far in advance who had to be advised of our planned absence and for whom we arranged alternative accommodation.

Our intention at that time was to go and live in the flat for up to a year; actually, it had to be either six months or a year as these were the durations of the tenancy agreements suggested by the agents we'd engaged to find our tenant. And of course, until we had the tenant, we felt that we couldn't leave, especially as the rental income was intended to contribute towards our travel and adventure expenses.

ii

Having placed the house for rental we were at a bit of a loose end so decided to fulfil another ambition. This was a trip to Amsterdam with dear friends Jill and Clive. Marilyn had been before in her early travelling days and it had been something we'd wanted to do together. I'd also had a fancy to visit one of the licensed 'coffee shops' and with my police service well behind me, sample a little legal 'whacky baccy'.

Going away with Jill and Clive is always fun as we often manage to find interesting places to stay and/or visit and this trip was no exception. I think it was Jill who came up with the idea of the barge. Of the many places to stay in Amsterdam from top-notch hotels to the most basic hostel, the former river barges converted for floating tourist accommodation certainly captured our imagination and we weren't disappointed. These are no small craft but huge cargo barges designed for the movement of substantial cargoes throughout the Netherlands to and from the major ports of Rotterdam and Amsterdam.

The one we booked was moored about a mile or so out of the centre and an easy walk or tram ride from the main areas of interest. The guest accommodation was self-contained and extremely well converted with the original main cargo area altered to provide a spacious sitting/dining area with a kitchenette and the whole space could easily be converted to an outside experience by sliding the huge loading hatch to one side.

There were also two very spacious en-suite bedrooms plus to the aft the owners own accommodation. It was a unique and novel creation, albeit one of many converted in the same way.

We must have walked miles around the city, crossing and re-crossing the canals. What a fantastic and very different space it is with so much less traffic but loads of bikes. I loved the canals, the gabled buildings, the absence of vehicle noise, much cleaner air and the whole ambience of the place.

We did go for numerous cups of coffee but in the end, I didn't pluck up the courage to try a bit of weed and I guess the moment has now passed (or maybe not) Should a 'baby boomer' actually depart this life without having smoked a bit of dope? I'll park that thought for the moment.

However, we did go exploring, including a brief excursion into the edge of the city's famous red-light district and what an eye-opener that was. With prostitution legal, the delights of the flesh were very much in your face at every corner and in every shape and size. Quite a revelation but you probably get the picture so enough said.

We did have one funny experience though when it started to rain. I decided to buy an umbrella so wandered into a shop and came out with a nice little black number with some kind of 'green decorative pattern'. It was only after we'd been wandering along the street for a while that Marilyn started laughing. She said *"I've seen it all now. A former police inspector wandering around Amsterdam with an umbrella decorated with cannabis leaves"*

iii

It took quite a while to find the tenant and we then immediately made our ferry reservations and the date was fixed. I must be a bit naïve but it never ceases to amaze me how sly some people can be when it comes to property and money and we discovered that the rental sector is no different to the house buying one with all its gazumping and so on.

The prospective tenants had negotiated us down quite considerably on the price, knowing I guess that we were planning to get away. However once agreed we thought that was it but right at the last minute, they said they wanted to pay even less and threatened to pull out. We were left with virtually no choice but to acquiesce and accept the lower figure as we were all booked and ready to go.

You wouldn't want to know the language we used about them. But seriously, it didn't leave a very pleasant taste or a feeling of great comfort about leaving them in our home – even though it was unfurnished and all our personal stuff was well away in store.

So anyway, there we were in October 2006, six years on from our first serious sortie into Spain and once again driving south to sample the Mediterranean lifestyle. Albeit this time with the family dog on board and the slightly more realistic agenda of a fixed (more or less) timescale rather than our great forever plan.

Living in the flat was so easy and autumn is such a lovely time on the Costa Brava especially as by that time there are not that many tourists around. Our previous visits had familiarized us with many of the local amenities and attractions and so initially we just dropped straight into holiday mode which was great. We chilled out, organized a telephone line to get internet in the flat, walked the promenade, found our way around the local supermarkets and incredibly I even ventured into the gym down at the Club Nautic in the marina. That didn't last. No surprise there.

Although we knew our way around the area a bit, further exploring became our main activity in those initial weeks. I've already mentioned the beautiful lake at Banyoles which became pretty much a regular once a week destination as did many of the small, achingly beautiful and unspoilt villages dotted all over the countryside. There you could come upon the small family-run restaurants where an excellent and wholesome *menu del dia* could be found for as little as eight or ten Euros including three courses, bread, wine and coffee. The giveaway for a good place to stop was always the number of local cars parked outside around lunchtime.

Dining habits I found were so civilized with a very leisurely lunch taken any time between about one and three o'clock. If we were actually at home, we even got into the siesta practice which left people fed and suitably refreshed to return to the shop or office around half four or five for the evening session before returning home via the local bar for a light dinner around nine or half-past. At weekends these times were usually a bit later and the sessions longer.

iv

However, we can only do holiday mode for a short time so quite soon we began to think about ways we could introduce a bit of structure to our lives. Our Spanish by then was more than adequate for day to day living like shopping, banking, ordering meals etc.

So, in addition to filling our time with some structured activity, we wanted to put ourselves in situations where we would need to use the language more. Although I previously mentioned the issues around Catalan being widely spoken, the situation in Empuriabrava was somewhat different because it is a resort. So while the locals usually speak Catalan between themselves, they will very easily and happily respond in Castellano with visitors, along with English, German, French and even the odd word of Russian too.

Marilyn decided to extend her Spanish proactively and enrolled in a language school in Gerona. Fortunately, she quickly discovered that there were several other people from our town on the course and so she was able to enter into a car-sharing arrangement with them which meant she only had to drive on every fourth day. The others were a Russian girl whose name I don't remember; crazy driver Pavlina from the Czech Republic who ran a pizzeria with her husband and Monique from Germany who we are still slightly in touch with.

For my part I decided to try to make use of my English teaching qualification, but where to start? Marilyn's new acquaintance Monique was already doing some English teaching and suggested I enquire at the same place. The Athena language school was a private venture run by Neus, a very stylish woman of somewhat indeterminate age but who was probably older than her style attempted to suggest. She was perfectly charming, made me very welcome and offered me two hours twice a week with four teenagers whose parents were paying for them to have extra English.

I approached this conscientiously with lesson plans and what I thought might prove interesting activities but frankly, I was on a loser from the start. Why? The class comprised four boys and one stunningly attractive girl. They were all about fifteen years of age with their hormones at full flow so you might imagine what the class dynamic was like. They were there because the parents had sent them but they didn't have the slightest interest in what I had to say. I think I did it for about four weeks and then told Neus I'd had enough. She wasn't surprised and it turned out that several other teachers had tried before me with a similar result so after hearing that I didn't feel so inadequate.

She then offered me a one-to-one class with a businessman. He was in construction and needed English for business. Naturally, his motivation was extremely high and we got on very well and continued for several weeks.

I also wondered whether I might be able to find someone who would pay me for one-to-one English teaching and Marilyn came up with the idea of posting adverts on local language school notice boards. As an alternative to paid classes, we framed the advert to also offer *'intercambio"* or exchange sessions so that I could also improve my Spanish and as a result, we met Cristina and Fernando who have become firm friends.

Christmas was a bit strange because as I explained previously it is not celebrated so enthusiastically out there. We missed our families terribly, although to be fair it was better than when we were in Vic because the nationalities present in Empuriabrava included a few Brits and quite a lot of French and German families. So as a result, the bars and shops were actually quite festive with various imported versions of Christmas Cheer.

We celebrated Christmas in the flat together with a lot of wine, half a roast turkey and the traditional trimmings and thought of family and friends doing the same at home. Half a turkey because we didn't have the fridge or freezer space to keep it and the kind butcher in Figueres agreed to keep the other half for as long as we wanted. I think we eventually had it at Easter.

Pablo's family in La Coruna had invited us for New Year so we packed up the car, put Robbie into some very good local kennels we'd found and headed off to drive 1216 kilometres (799 miles) right across Spain. It's funny really because there is no way we would have considered going more than a couple of hundred miles at the most for a party here in England but one quickly gets used to the fact that in a large country, it's what you do. We Brits can be a bit parochial I think.

There was a great welcome for us with Cristina and Juan, grandmother, Pablo and his brother Pedro. It was just like visiting family. I think we had about three days there where we celebrated the New Year with bubbly and ate the traditional twelve grapes at midnight. The idea is to eat one with every chime of the midnight hour. Easier said than done but a lot of fun trying.

Then as if such a journey were nothing at all we were back on the road to our flat where we had Three Kings festivities on 6th January.

Although it seemed on one level eerily strange to be in a holiday resort in mid-winter with virtually no visitors, on another it was very pleasant if a little surreal as we wandered around the seafront with no-one else in sight. The best thing though was that unlike the grey winter skies we are accustomed to here in the UK, out there for the majority of time, while seriously cold sometimes, we were almost always under blue skies. It's the light isn't it that most people miss during the English winter months.

From winter into spring we enjoyed life in the flat, walking every day with the dog in the immediate surroundings and in the nature reserve areas that adjoin both sides of Empuriabrava. Several times a week we ventured further afield as there were still quite a few places we hadn't discovered. I think it was also about this time that we discovered the British Catalunya Society. As the name suggests it is an organization of UK ex-pats living in the area and its principal objective seemed to be social which was just what we needed. Although to be honest our original hope was that we would find our social interaction with locals rather than the ex-pat community. My own effort was through the teaching but Marilyn was a bit braver and joined a local class making ceramic jewellery. But the bottom line was that we just weren't locals and our language skills were too limited for easy integration. Not that they were rude but she just didn't feel comfortable.

However, the BCS was welcoming and the first event we attended turned out to be a car treasure hunt. It was quite good fun even though we got hopelessly lost and decamped to a local bar from where we observed various other competitors driving to and fro apparently equally lost. We were last home but it didn't matter. We went to a couple of other events where it became pretty clear that the social element was mostly concerned with committees, gossip and alcohol which was sad as we had some hopes there. However, we did meet Dave and Evie, an English couple who were living in Figueres and have become good long-term friends. They, like us, eventually called it a day and having had the 'foreign living' experience, are now back here in the UK.

Spring comes early in this part of the world and so in February there were acres of cherry blossom to be admired in the area inland from Figueres and here we also discovered more lovely little villages clustered around tumbling streams fed by the melting snow of the lower slopes. Higher up the snow persists for longer and supports a busy winter sports centre in Vall de Nuria.
However, it doesn't have the altitude of other better known European ski resorts and has struggled a bit in the last few years due to climate change and insufficient snowfall.

Undoubtedly worth a visit, Vall de Núria sits 3000 metres above sea level in a perfect little valley hidden from view, until the last moment, by the mountains which surround it. In the centre of the valley lies a quite austere building that looks more like it should be lining a plaza in Eastern

Europe. In a way it adds to the impact, contrasting against emerald pastures and the sparkling blue lake that lies calmly in front of it. The building contains a hotel, exhibition centre and restaurants and is the focal point for many activities in the Vall de Núria.

Marilyn in the snow – Vall de Nuria

Even getting there is an experience. A rack railway climbs 12.5km from Ribes de Freser via Queralbs through the sort of wild mountain scenery that would make the journey alone worth the price of a ticket. For the last few minutes, the train runs in a tunnel emerging dramatically into the light at the last moment on the lake's edge. That's the easy way up. Mountain paths lead through stunning countryside to the valley. It's a tough climb though and it's probably better to enjoy the train journey up and then walk down. I'll confess that we took the train both ways although if Marilyn had been alone, she would probably have walked it one way or the other.

Winter or summer, Vall de Nuria has much to offer the mountain enthusiast thanks to the beautiful scenery, clean air, wildflowers, high-level walks or a variety of ski runs.

You probably won't be surprised the read that the more time we spent exploring the country our thoughts began again to turn to the possibility of making a life there. I know this will sound crazy given our previous experience but that's the way it was and we started to wonder if perhaps the purchase of something in the Galicia region where properties were ridiculously cheap (by UK standards) might be worth considering. Looking online we'd seen any number of rural properties for sale, mostly needing fairly significant restoration but even so, extremely cheap and so we decided to have another look.

In the summer when the Costa Brava gets very hot and busy we prefer not to be there so around the beginning of July we packed the car up and headed out and right across the country to Galicia again. As I've said we had friends there, namely Anna and Lluis in delightfully rural Cristosende and Pablo's family in La Coruna and while we fully intended to touch base with them both we wanted to be a little independent too.

To this end, we found a pretty stone holiday cottage to let on the banks of the River Sil canyon. We were on the north, i.e., south-facing side in amongst the many hectares of vines with a dramatic view of the river and the heavily wooded hillside opposite.

The view from our rented cottage

It truly was the most idyllic situation imaginable and suited us perfectly as a base for exploring the area further whilst being within reach for visiting the friends. As the crow flies it was barely a mile or so from Anna and Lluis' place in Cristosende which was higher up and on the other side of the canyon. The journey to them was tortuous, requiring an ascent from our location, a five-mile drive before descending again to the bridge and then climbing back up to them. It was a bit like I remember Scotland in that respect – you need to go a long way to get a short distance.

The nearest town of any size was Montforte de Lemos, an historic and attractive place under a looming castle. This would be our main venue for any significant shopping although there was also the much smaller village of Sober with just one mini-market, church, school and a couple of café-bars.

From Sober, a challenging narrow road wound steeply down the canyon sides to the tiny hamlet of Portobrosmos comprising just five houses including ours.

On arrival, we went straight through the living room, down a spiral staircase and out onto a small patio overlooking the vines that sloped down to the river a hundred feet or so below. Beside the patio which was supplied with sun loungers and parasols, a pretty al-fresco barbecue and eating area had a set of table and chairs and the whole was delightfully shaded by a rampant vine laden with grapes.

There were neighbours in the next-door garden when we arrived and we learnt that they were from Monforte and this was their holiday/weekend cottage. They were wonderfully friendly and the following evening invited us round for a barbecue where we met another neighbour from the house opposite. He turned out to be a retired policeman like myself so we had no shortage of conversation which was just what we needed to extend our vocabulary and improve language skills. He owned quite a large area of vines and was living in the hamlet during the season to tend and in due course pick the grapes. A couple of days later we and the other neighbours went to his place for drinks and barbecued sardines. Lovely!

We arranged with a local agent to have a look at some houses. Loads of ancient granite and chestnut wood. So full of character and usually with outbuildings and a bit of land and predictably I guess our imaginations were running riot. A couple of days later Pablo's parents Cristina and Juan came down from La Coruna to visit and accompany us on a couple more viewings. It was certainly helpful to have them on hand and they were able to ask more questions than our language ability allowed. It soon became clear that if we were once again to consider going down this road, we would have to be very careful because every property we looked at that ticked our 'characterful' requirement also ticked a pretty large restoration bill.

Whilst driving around we had noticed that there seemed to be an unusual number of hikers and in Portomarin where we had stopped at a shop, there were quite a number in the square taking on board refreshment, airing some sore looking feet and generally taking some time out before kitting up and heading off again. We were puzzled and I went and spoke to a guy to see if I could discover a bit more.

He turned out to be a sixty-year-old recently retired engineer from Toronto and he explained he was walking the 'Camino de Santiago', the ancient pilgrim route to the shrine of St James in the city of Santiago de

Compostela in Galicia. He explained he had walked from the Pyrenees which was a little over four hundred miles away. Apparently, he had never walked before, at least not any serious distance, but having heard about the route he was just captivated by the idea of having some time out *to 'get my head together'* as he put it just after retiring from his business life. We were fascinated but little did we know the significance of that encounter for our future lives.

Whenever we've talked about the possibility of living or spending longer periods in Spain, and because, as I've said, we don't do holiday mode for long; we have always considered possible occupations. The same question occupied our minds then as we wondered about buying a Galician house. It was (as usual) Marilyn who came up with the idea that given our first-hand experience as accommodation providers with our B&B, we might set up a hostel for pilgrims walking the Camino.

It was around this time that our agents told us that our tenants had given notice to terminate the tenancy early. So with a sudden reduction in our funding, we made plans for an immediate return and arrived back in Peaslake towards the end of July 2007.

Robbie helps with the unpacking back in Peaslake

13   HOME AGAIN

i

Just like before; picking up life back in Peaslake was so easy and in no time, it seemed almost as though we had never been away.

My mothballed handyman enterprise came easily back to life and after republishing the parish magazine advert and a little local networking, word soon spread and the work started to come in. Fortunately, Marilyn was able to return on a part-time basis to the tourist office in Guildford; we reopened The Garden Room for B&B guests and before long that was off and running again too.

The families I had been driving for were more than happy to see me back and available and one couple who employed me regularly for their domestic running around also started to use me for business. They ran a marketing enterprise and did a fair amount of business entertaining that often involved eating and drinking in posh London restaurants and at events like the Goodwood Revival. My role was to drive them and/or their clients to and from the venues.

Apart from the concentration needed for the actual driving it was pretty mindless and mundane really and having to listen to the heavily jargonized business-speak was mind-numbing to be truthful and all the more so on the way back from events when they were all well-oiled and to my mind were all talking mostly complete bollocks. However, the money was pretty good for not a lot of effort.

I also contacted Savills to see if perhaps I could resume my work with them. The admin element of the job I had done had been taken back into the office and was run very competently by one of their staff. However, they were more than happy for me to go back to the copy-writing as it saved their negotiators the task of making a further visit to properties to write the sales descriptions.

These activities didn't occupy all of our time and it wasn't long before Marilyn started to need more and she found a part-time job at the local hotel in our village. The job was receptionist/duty manager which was eminently suited to her highly organized approach and attention to detail. She got on extremely well with Sherril the manager and soon became a valued part of that team.

In October Marilyn had a significant birthday so by way of celebration we went off to Venice – for a day! I grant it seems a bit extravagant which it was, but it was such fun and despite the rain a very memorable experience.

On the water taxi to St Mark's Square, Venice

ii

A couple of other things happened for me in those last two months of 2007; namely two new interests developed which were to become quite significant parts of my life in the years ahead. These were photography and writing.

Although I was happy that the handyman activity had built up again so easily, I started to feel the need for another interest that would be more of a hobby than a commercial activity. I think too that I was starting to get a bit bored with the relatively unchallenging nature of most of the handyman stuff. The jobs were usually pretty simple and few required much ingenuity just a bit of know-how and the right tools both of which I had but I desperately needed something else.

I had always had an interest in photography although the family and career-building in the police had kept that interest pretty much in the background. When digital first arrived, I had a couple of very cheap compact cameras thereby keeping myself a bit familiar with that development. Anyway, I decided that this was to be my new hobby and started to read around the subject with a view to getting myself a more serious camera with greater potential.

Looking at several reviews in different photographic magazines (bearing in mind that the internet back then was not the information and comparison resource it is today) I decided that I needed an SLR (single-lens reflex) camera and that I would definitely stick with digital because of the immediacy it offered. I was pretty hooked on computer technology anyway as that had been a major component of my last few years in the Police.

I didn't have a lot of money to spend so I bought the small Nikon D40X which was then more or less an entry-level camera. However, compared to the little digital compact it was a real 'all singing and dancing' piece of kit that would allow a far greater degree of control for some more creative photography. Well, that's pretty much what the sales pitch said; all I had to do was to find my way around what to me at first appeared a pretty complicated set of buttons and dials.

It was probably around this time that another new interest began. Memoir writing. Well, it didn't begin in such a fully formed way but rather evolved over a long time.

I can't put an exact date on it but I can clearly remember hearing myself say one day (possibly to the kids) *"I can hardly remember anything about my young life."* And then I can remember thinking *"That's crazy. I just need to try harder."*

So began a personal challenge to see what I could actually remember and write a few things down. Now I do tend to be quite methodical once I take something on and this was how I approached the 'memory lane' exercise.

I'd done brainstorming at work on various occasions and so I decided to use the same technique but as a solo exercise when it is known as mind-mapping. I took a large sheet of paper, drew a small circle and in it wrote down two words *"Bramley Way"* - the road I grew up in. I then drew short lines to a dozen other circles where I wrote other words triggered by *Bramley Way.* These included *parents, friends, neighbours, house, garden, school, village, church, Ashtead Park* and so on. Each of these new words was then used to trigger further memories and once begun the process produced a veritable avalanche of memory notes. But what now?

I think the original idea was simply to do the exercise to prove I could, but then I began to think it might be quite nice to pull it all together into a kind of memory archive that could be interesting for its own sake and maybe even for the kids. However, I had no real idea about how I might collate the thing but rather than leave it simply as a bunch of notes in a lever file I thought that maybe I could create a memoir.

To progress this idea, I joined a writing group in Guildford to get some help with structure, layout and so on. Each week we took along a piece of writing that we read to the group to get feedback and advice from the tutor. Hearing that some of the other group members had actually written and published their work, that became my next goal. The idea of holding a professionally bound and produced volume and say *"I did this."* was just so appealing although I certainly didn't see it as a commercial possibility.

However, my fellow students were very encouraging, laughed at all my escapades and the general view seemed to be that I should try to get it published. Even Jane Baker our tutor said I seemed to have *'found my voice'.*

Now please don't run away with the idea that this all happened just like that in a short time because it absolutely did not; in fact, it was some seven years coming off and on the back burner as other activities took precedence or my interest was otherwise diverted.

iii

In parallel with all the above, travel was still a big item on our agenda whenever possible which included the Spanish flat even for just a few days.

We certainly became good customers for Ryanair or EasyJet depending on which one could fly us to Barcelona or Girona for the cheapest price. Seen against today's environmental issues I do have a pang of conscience when I think about the air or motorway miles we clocked up, but then no different to millions of others and certainly less than many.

A great photographic opportunity came up in December of 2007 when we decided to take a trip to Italy's Amalfi Coast and include the ancient sites of Pompeii and Herculaneum. I had been to Naples once before in 1962 when the P&O cruise ship I was working on called in there. I didn't like what I saw of Naples then and spent my whole day off enjoying a trip out to Capri in the bay.

I guess most people know the history of how on Thursday 24th August AD79 Mount Vesuvius erupted, destroying and burying the two Roman cities under metres of ash and lava. However, nothing quite prepares one for the stark reality of the petrified bodies caught and killed where they stood by the fast-moving pyroclastic flows before being entombed beneath the ash.

The scale of the subsequent archaeology has been no less impressive considering the quantity of material that has been removed over the years to reveal the buried cities and minute detail of the everyday lives lived there. Following the stone-paved streets furrowed by years of cartwheels and looking into the exposed shops and houses, it almost felt as though the people had just "popped out" and would be back shortly. December was a good time to be there as there were few visitors and the atmosphere was stronger for that.

In February '08 we were back to the flat for the Calçot Fiesta. I kid you not, this could only happen in Spain where they will have a fiesta on the slightest pretext. Calçots are a vegetable like a thin leek or large spring onion and the fiesta is a community event that involves eating these and drinking wine. As I said – any excuse for a party – seems to be the maxim in Spain.

The calçots (pronounced calzots) are harvested in February and on the fiesta day, which happens in many villages, tables are set up along the streets and the calçots are barbecued. Whole villages turn out with family and friends. For a small fee, each visitor receives about ten wrapped in newspaper along with a plastic cup of wine, chunks of rustic bread and a little pot of spicy sauce together with a plastic bib.

You then take these to a table where you secure your space and get started. The method is to peel off any overly burnt skin, dip your calçot in the sauce and eat it along with your bread and wine. The problem is there is no cutlery and the calçots are soft and floppy, so the only realistic way to do it is to hold it up high and lower it into your mouth. This is why the bib is required. These fiestas are huge if rather messy fun but all the more entertaining for that and because everyone gets messy together, they are a great leveller and do masses to cement community relations.

In the main street of nearby Vila Sacra with friend Fernando on the left getting to grips with his slippery Calçots whilst Marilyn opposite chats with friend Cristina.

I previously described how our young Spanish friend Pablo had come to stay with us and gained an English teaching qualification; well in March, we heard that his world had moved on somewhat.

He had obviously taken our conversations to heart about perhaps having to leave Spain to get the teaching experience his CV so badly needed. It turned out that he had made some enquiries about such possibilities and been offered three years teaching in Chicago. We were stunned that he had been bold enough to do it as we were certain his parents wouldn't have been keen, but we were also thrilled to see this young man mustering his courage to step out beyond the rather sheltered environment of the typical Spanish family home.

Excited though we were on his behalf we were also rather concerned as to how he would manage and the posting could hardly have been further away. We also wondered who he would be teaching in the English-speaking USA. He explained that the school he was going to had a high proportion of Hispanic children and to minimize the ghettoization that can arise in immigrant communities; ensuring that the younger generation learnt English was seen as a priority.

So, in April, we went to see him. Marilyn had been to the States before in her independent travelling days courtesy of Freddy Laker in the seventies but it was my first time apart from the flying visits I made to the west coast while with P&O where I saw a lot of bars but learnt absolutely zero about the country. We found Pablo well-established in a rented flat and we were so impressed with what he had achieved. Apparently, he had been given a week after arrival to get his bearings, find some accommodation and fix himself up with a car, all of which he appeared to have achieved with relative ease.

Pablo took us to his school and this is taken in his classroom

I had never been keen on visiting the US fearing that it would reinforce all my negative stereotypes as big, brash, noisy, and polluted. Frankly, it was all those things but it was also totally fascinating and the people were so friendly.

Pablo lived in a town called Elgin in the suburbs of Chicago and fortunately was able to take a little time out to show us around a bit. We did the usual touristy things like going up the Sears Tower, riding the L line, walking the city's Lake Michigan waterfront, shopping in Macy's, visited an 'Old West' frontier encampment mock-up complete with fort and chuckwagon and following the Frank Lloyd Wright architectural trail.

Probably one of the most enjoyable experiences for me was visiting a downtown blues bar and it took me right back to 1962 when I was with P&O and we called into San Francisco. One evening we visited the legendary Jazz Workshop where I was privileged to hear the great jazz saxophonists John Coltrane and Stan Getz playing together. Dark, smoky and just so chilled it was at once one of the most relaxing and exciting moments of my life. So reliving that memory was lovely.

View from the top of the Willis (formerly Sears) Tower – 1450ft

14   MORE OF EVERYTHING

i

It wasn't as if we weren't doing an interesting variety of things because we were and frankly a lot of the time it seemed our feet were hardly touching the ground.

The Garden Room B&B was still trundling along very successfully; I was still copy-writing for Savills and their expensive houses and am bound to say enjoying it greatly. I always fancied the high life and if I couldn't own it, dipping my toe and nose in and out of other people's homes was fascinating.
I was still being a handyman as well as chauffeuring rich kids and their parents around the place. We had an idyllic lifestyle in a lovely part of the world but somehow for me, something was beginning to pall.

I'm not sure what it was; a kind of superficiality perhaps; a sense that whilst quite well occupied I wasn't really achieving a lot. I even considered looking for a full time employed job. The problem there was that I had no idea what that might be and perhaps mainly that, when the chips were down, after being my own boss for the last fourteen years since leaving the police, I just couldn't contemplate working to someone else's timetable and rules.

One day whilst (unusually for me) browsing the local paper, I spotted an advert for drivers. This was for an agency that put drivers into several local car dealerships around Surrey on an 'as required' basis. Similar to the way that Harwoods at Pulborough had employed drivers on a casual basis or what we would now call 'zero hours contracts'; this agency had up to a couple of dozen drivers it could call on and put into local businesses when needed. This might have been to cover busy times, leave or sickness, but there had been an increasing trend for companies to fully outsource various services and this was just another that was coming under that umbrella.

I applied and once again the 'ex-police driver' history worked its magic and I got the job. Some weeks I could find myself working in two or three local dealerships but the best was a posting to an almost full-time job covering sickness at the Guildford Porsche Centre.

As you might imagine I was in seventh heaven driving some of those cars. However, like most things I guess, the euphoria didn't last, mainly because a thrill is only a thrill if it is occasional but also because some of the owners were so damn precious about their beloved cars and exhibited such a lack of trust it really got on our nerves. I guess if I had spent tens of thousands or sometimes much more on a car, I would want to make sure it was treated well but some were just a bit too much.

This situation continued for several months and apart from the frustrations mentioned it worked very well and provided the flexibility I loved whilst topping up the pension to fund our travels.

ii

We had a great local farm shop at Abinger and one day I was in there and casually browsing the notice board when I saw another job that caught my eye. An occasional driver was required to chauffeur a company CEO on an ad-hoc basis. Good references and driving experience were a must, both of which I had.

The position would be based at the client's home address near Guildford and the requirement would be for a variety of shifts varying from a couple of hours to long days and some evenings for social events. There might be a requirement to work a week or more continuously or perhaps not be required for a week or so at a time. That suited my needs perfectly so I picked up the phone and spoke to James Harding.

To my amazement, he took me on immediately solely based on a ten-minute conversation. It turned out that he lived very close by in Albury and was the CEO of a company headquartered in Byfleet near Woking.

Now here comes the coincidence. Jim Harding was a lovely man and turned out to be a former primary school friend of mine. We were in the same class at St Peter's in Leatherhead. Curious how far our paths had diverged and then reunited more than fifty years on.

The car I had to drive was a super luxurious Mercedes saloon. Fast when necessary, comfortable and with all the bells and whistles you'd ever want so it was a dream to drive and great to sit around in for hours which I had to do quite often.

Over the following few weeks and months, I came to know Jim's family and went to his home often where I was always made most welcome. No one stood on any ceremony.

At the time I first started working for Jim he was in the process of preparing the company for some major commercial venture I didn't really understand. Not that he specifically discussed any detail with me but he was quite keen to talk as we drove when he wasn't on the phone or deep in some paperwork in the back. In this connection, I spent a lot of time driving him around London where he had meetings, presentations and the like.

Jim was always thin as a rake but I noticed after a while that he had started to look positively gaunt and on one occasion he came out of a meeting and was immediately violently sick in the back of the car. He didn't want to stop for any help or see a doctor so I was hardly surprised that a couple of days later I learnt that he had been rushed to hospital and was more or less in a critical condition.

It turned out that he had undiagnosed gluten intolerance and had been ignoring symptoms for so long that his whole body chemistry was a mess and he very nearly died. Thankfully he heeded the warning from the event itself and also from his doctors that he needed to take things easy so he put in train his retirement intending to enjoy his family and all the lovely things his hard work over the years had enabled. I stopped driving him of course and apart from a Christmas card and a bottle that he brought round to our house himself we more or less lost contact.

It was only a few months later when I was deeply saddened to hear that

Jim had died. He had been diagnosed with aggressive Lymphoma and had died within weeks of its discovery.

I must say it did tend to put life in perspective concerning what one should regard as important – business success or personal and family life. He worked so hard; it was tragic that in the end, he was unable to enjoy more of the benefits. As they say *"Money isn't everything."* Jim Harding – a perfect gentleman, taken far too soon.

iii

Despite the best of intentions, my photography had been on the back burner and the various dials and buttons on the still hardly touched new camera remained a mystery. I decided a positive move was needed so I signed up for a course – *Introduction to digital photography* – at West Dean College.

The college was not new to me as I had previously done at least three woodworking courses there and I was quite in love with the atmosphere and location that was so calm and conducive to learning.

The main thing I learnt was that a modern digital SLR camera can be as simple or complex as the user wishes. Leave it on fully automatic mode and it will produce nice photos allowing the owner to simply point and compose the image. But, the central thrust of the course was to get us away from the Auto mode; then to take greater control of the camera to get the picture you want rather than the one the camera manufacturer wants to give you.

Following the course in June, I took myself off for ten days to Scotland to put what I'd learnt into practice. I flew up to Inverness, hired a car and drove along the Great Glen beside Loch Ness to Fort William on the west coast. Stopping in a variety of B&B's, I went out to Skye and then up the coast as far as Durness and Cape Wrath in the far north-west.

I can recall one evening sitting on the beach near Plockton and taking a hundred or more photos of the same scene, changing the settings to suit the fading light. By the end of the day, I had a fair idea of the Aperture – Exposure – ISO triangle theory.

One of my objectives on the trip had been to visit the mile-long beach at Sandwood Bay which requires a longish walk from the nearest vehicle access. Unfortunately, on the day I arrived the wind was blowing a gale and the rain was horizontal which sadly made the plan impossible.

I continued up to Durness and along the north coast to a lovely B&B overlooking Loch Eribol. It is one of the deeper sea lochs and has been used for centuries as a safe anchorage away from the turbulent waters around Cape Wrath and the Pentland Firth. Eribol also has an interesting military history.

The little island I overlooked from my B&B room had been used during the Second World War as a substitute for the German battleship Tirpitz and used for bombing practice by the Fleet Air Arm before the successful Operation Tungsten in April 1944.

The following year as the war ended in 1945, Eribol was also the place where the surviving thirty-three U-boats of the German Atlantic fleet surrendered to English forces.

Returning from this trip I was enthused with photographic fervour and immediately embarked on a veritable orgy of landscape photography in and around the Surrey Hills. I gathered a huge archive of local Surrey Hills landscape images to the point where I pretty well ran out of places to photograph, at least within a few miles of where we lived. Landscape was my main interest for a long time although I also enjoyed historic buildings and all types of architecture.

This is one of my very early landscapes taken on Holmbury Hill. Sadly, this black and white version doesn't do it justice.

Like most artists I guess, satisfying myself was only part of the process as there was also a need-to-know what others thought of what I was doing. To that end, in today's online world there are fortunately many ways in which artists of all types can share and enjoy each-others efforts. The one I chose initially was Flickr and for several years I continued to enjoy posting my work and viewing other's.

Of course, I also enjoyed the complimentary remarks about some of my pictures. But after a while, I started to feel that it was a bit of a mutual admiration society where it was only too easy both give and receive brief compliments like *"great shot", "super image", "good work"* or even just the one-worders like *"Awesome"*

In truth, it became pretty meaningless and I would have loved for someone to say *"love this shot but had you thought of trying......"* A bit of constructive criticism is worth a thousand Well Done's.

I guess I must have some innate commercial instincts because I find it hard not to think about ways in which my efforts might earn me a few bob and the same thing happened with my landscape photography.

This was largely due to the praise I received for the images I shared online and I came to wonder how I could make it work for me. I came up with greeting cards. Actually, it would be more truthful to say that several people suggested that my landscapes would make nice cards so I started to look into the possibilities.

For any commercial venture, it is achieving a low enough unit production cost that is key if one is going to be able to sell and make a worthwhile return. When it came to card printing, most companies would only consider runs of 200 minimum per image which was a bit tricky as I had no idea initially who I might be able to sell them to.

I mean I could hardly go into a local shop and say *"Look, I've got this card."* Clearly, I needed to be able to offer a range, but how many? If, for example, I selected an initial range of ten different images that would have meant I would have had a couple of thousand cards without knowing who might buy them and frankly I'm not that much of a speculator. This statement does rather fly in the face of my entrepreneurial claims so I suppose I must fall somewhere in between.

I mulled this conundrum over for a long while and had more or less concluded that having them commercially printed was not going to be a runner at least not to start with and I guess to some extent the idea went on my personal back burner. But not my dear wife's, although she didn't say anything at the time.

iv

It seemed that greeting cards were not the only thing on Marilyn's mind because she said one day *"Would you mind if I wanted to go and walk the Camino de Santiago?"* Well, it was a bit of a surprise because apart from referring back a few times to our meeting with the walkers in Galicia we hadn't until then discussed the idea of her doing the walk.

I certainly didn't mind and even if I did, I had no right to make any objection. My only concern was her safety and more particularly her ability as she had never done any significant long distances and certainly not on numerous consecutive days, nor was she keen on hills at the best of times.

Marilyn had been more than a little impressed with the walkers and had started to read up and find out more about the Camino. It is an ancient pilgrim route that has been walked for more than a thousand years by Christians wishing to pay homage at the bones of St James the Apostle.

How his remains came to be there more than 800 years after he was martyred by Herod in the Holy Land in 44AD is a matter of conjecture. However, it is believed, and perhaps with some basis, that following Jesus' instruction to the Disciples to *"go ye therefore and teach all nations ..."* Saint James headed west and arrived in Spain where he preached in the north-west corner which is present-day Galicia after which he returned to meet his fate in Jerusalem. The following summarises the history better than I could: -

Mystery, legend and colourful myths are all part of the history of the Camino.

According to the official history of the pilgrimage, the body of Saint James the Apostle, son of Zebedee and brother of John the Evangelist, was discovered by a shepherd named Pelayo in a field in Galicia during the reign of King Alfonso II, back in the 9th century. The Apostle gives the route its name: Camino de Santiago means the Way of Saint James; Santiago or Sant Iago meaning Saint James.

Saint James had died some 800 years earlier and according to legend was transported to Galicia (to the town of Iria Flavia, today's Padron, on the Camino Portugues) by two disciples in a boat led by angels. Somehow his body was then buried in a field not far from there; where it would be discovered a few centuries later.

Informed about this important discovery, King Alfonso II had a small chapel built in this holy place and would later commission a larger temple to attract pilgrims from all over the world, competing with other important religious centres of pilgrimage such as Jerusalem and Rome. Of course, at this time, religious buildings across Europe were busy competing for the best relics, as a way of attracting pilgrims, and the relics of Saint James would transform Santiago de Compostela into one of the world's most important pilgrimage destinations. (Credit for the above paragraphs is due to www.caminoways.com(Cynical aside from me – what is it they say about not letting the truth get in the way of a good story or commercial opportunity?)

Marilyn had read a lot around the Camino pilgrimage and while not especially religious herself in any traditional sense she had a strong urge to travel the route as it was certainly clear that for many it had been quite a spiritual experience; described by some as being like a *"walking meditation"*.
I could certainly identify with that myself as I find solitude amidst the beauty of nature and wild places touches me in a way I can easily describe as spiritual.

As I said, I was a bit concerned about the safety element of her proposal but Marilyn is an experienced solo traveller and the more we studied the route it became apparent that the main route – the Camino Frances, has a plentiful supply of regularly spaced accommodation for pilgrims and is a well-travelled path. It was always her intention to walk alone but it was clear that she was unlikely to ever be totally isolated. It seemed then that the only thing remaining was for her to get walking fit and she set to this task with determination.

This preparation included frequent day hikes within striking distance of home, either alone or with her main walking friend Juliette. They also completed both The North and the South Downs Ways which are each over a hundred miles long. To enable them to do several consecutive days I was pressed into service as a taxi driver ferrying them to and from start points. The Thames Path and the Cotswold Way also fell to their efforts.

Meanwhile, between us we were still running the B&B; I was driving, copy-writing for the estate agents and still doing the occasional bit of handyman stuff. Marilyn was also working at the hotel.

In July 2008 my brother-in-law Hugh died and in August I went down to spend some time with my sister Angela in Gloucestershire. I found this a very precious time and whilst sad I discovered a closeness with my sister I hadn't known previously.

Any spare minutes saw me charging around the local countryside capturing landscape images and then in September we went back to the flat in Empuriabrava to enjoy the annual Troubadours Festival in the historic old town of Castello. Christmas came and went followed by a very cold couple of weeks at the beginning of January with some spectacular hoar frosts that provided some lovely photographic opportunities.

Whilst I had been down with my sister the previous August she had taken me to a very interesting place not far from her home. Angela lives in the village of Saul which is close to the Gloucester and Sharpness canal just south of the city of Gloucester and one day she took me to the old Sharpness docks.

I'm interested in our industrial heritage both from the historical perspective and more recently for the photographic opportunity it presents.

I love these gritty old industrial places for photography.

Gloucester was once a major port in the west of England and served shipping on the River Severn whose size was restricted by the navigational challenges of the river and the significant tidal range of the Severn that limited its use especially as ships became larger.

To overcome these problems a plan was devised in the late 18th Century to build a canal from Sharpness to Gloucester that would give deep-water access from the Severn estuary and bypass the hazardous bends and shifting sandbanks on the main river. At its opening in 1827, the twenty-six-and-a-half-mile canal was the broadest and deepest in the world and it maintained the commercial life of Gloucester docks for many years thereafter.

Angela had also told me about the Purton Ships Graveyard and so in February 2009 I went to visit her again and made a point of going down again to Sharpness.

In the early 20th Century, a problem arose at Purton where the canal runs very close to the main river and erosion was threatening to breach the narrow strip between the two. To halt the erosion, old and unwanted ships, barges and other river craft were beached along the banks which not only limited the erosion but actually reversed it by causing a build-up of silt and in effect rebuilding the land. This place is certainly worth a visit both for its history and the rather surreal impression it creates with the numerous old half-buried hulks of metal, wood and concrete sticking up from the sandy river banks and looking for all the world like the bones of so many long-dead sea monsters.

Old boat timbers at Purton Ships' Graveyard

As time moved on, increasingly larger ships became unable to navigate the canal. So new docks were constructed at Sharpness with appropriate road and rail connections that eventually reduced the canal traffic through Gloucester to the point where today it is used for little more than recreational boating.

v

A year or so later I took myself off for another landscape photography expedition to Scotland and when I arrived home Marilyn said *"I've had an idea about your greeting cards. What do you think of this?"* and with that, she produced a nice looking little A6 size card made with one of my landscape images.

It transpired that in my absence she had been talking to our friends Lola and Barbara who make greeting cards which they sell to make money for their church. They had taken Marilyn along to a craft shop they use and shown her these tri-fold card blanks with an aperture behind which a photo could be fixed and glued in place. The first and second panels are then glued together sandwiching the photo so that it appears through the aperture on the front face.

I had to admit it looked quite good but I said something like *"Yes it's nice but it's home-made."*

"No." she said *"It's hand-crafted and that's its selling point. Hand-made or hand-crafted is where it's at right now. People don't' want the mass-produced article so much these days. They like to feel a thing has been made with care rather than with a million others by a machine."*

Well, it was certainly a way of thinking I hadn't considered but I could see immediately that it might well be true and it would certainly solve the printing problem. There are numerous firms offering photo printing in any number and size you want and usually the more you order the less the unit cost is. The principle is pretty much similar to the digital print-on-demand set-up I mentioned earlier when talking about the book.

I did have a good enough printer to produce my own in fairly small numbers which is what I did to create a set of samples. It also meant that I was able to put together a small album showing forty or fifty different local landscape scenes from which I could invite potential customers to choose. I could then get these printed for as little as four pence an image. Adding in the cost of the card blank and envelope plus a cellophane bag I came to a final production cost per card of around 40 pence or a little more or less depending on the number I had printed at a time.

Armed with the samples album I set off around a few likely retail outlets and the first one was the Peaslake village shop. The ladies there were very supportive and enthusiastic and agreed to take an initial stock of fifty mixed cards. Sherril, the manager of the Hurtwood Inn hotel also took some as did one of the cafés and the gift shop in Shere. I also managed to get a shop in Cranleigh to accept a small stock so I was pretty well pleased. All I had to do then was produce them.

Once I'd ordered some two hundred and fifty card-size prints I spent my time very happily in my workshop tuned into Classic FM or Radio 4; mind in neutral, turning photos and card blanks into rather smart greeting cards complete with envelopes and cellophane wraps.

I guess taking into account all the production costs and my mark-up of almost a hundred per cent I made about forty to fifty pence a card for about 6 minutes work, which I sold to the retail outlets for ninety pence initially. They eventually retailed at about £1.60p so all in all everyone was happy and my work was out there and selling quite well which was hugely satisfying. My costing calculations had not factored in my own time to make the cards but it was only intended to be a hobby really and if it cleared the expenses and made a small margin, I was happy. It wasn't going to make my fortune but that wasn't the point.

The little project got a big boost when Marilyn took a few of the cards into the Tourist Office in Guildford. The manager there was really keen so I had to set to and add some Guildford images to the product range and was rewarded with their first order of two hundred cards which was so exciting. She even commissioned me to do a few local shots as page banners for their Guildford Tourism website including a credit to me as the photographer.

15   THE WAY OF ST JAMES

i

On the eighteenth of March 2009, Marilyn set out to walk the Camino de Santiago. Five hundred miles across Spain so I was a little apprehensive on her behalf and I know she was too. She had given notice at the Tourist Office and the hotel in the village but the hotel manager said she would hold the job for the ten weeks or so Marilyn was planning to be away which was pretty amazing and showed very clearly how well she was regarded there.

Marilyn was going to have the company of her friend Juliette for the first week and I took them to the airport for the flight to Biarritz. From there they had to get public transport to their start point which was the town of Roncesvalles just over the Spanish border in the Pyrenees.

The route Marilyn had planned is known as the Camino Frances because it comes into Spain over the mountains from France and is a continuation of the path through France where it is known as Chemin de St Jacques. There are many pilgrim routes to Santiago that converge on the city like the spokes of a wheel and some originate as far afield as northern Europe. Historically, medieval pilgrims from England used to start at Winchester then walk via Canterbury to the coast before crossing The Channel to pick up one of the French routes. The section Marilyn was planning to walk was about 500 miles (Yes, I couldn't believe the plan at first either!) but she was actually to meet people who had walked from Denmark and were then on the return leg!!

At first, I'd found the whole idea mind-boggling; that my dear wife could contemplate walking across Spain but by the time they were ready to go I guess I was kind of used to the idea.

The plan was that she would walk five days and then rest for one and also that she would plan her walking hours to be relatively short thereby hopefully avoiding blisters and any other physical problems. Unlike some walkers who are obliged to fit the trip into annual holidays, Marilyn had plenty of time. She felt that by allowing herself shorter walking hours she would arrive early enough at each *hostal* to be sure of accommodation and also have time to discover a little about the many fascinating places along the way.

Meanwhile, I was to carry on running the Garden Room and my other various activities for eight weeks and then head out to Galicia myself. We arranged to rent the same little cottage in the Sil Canyon where we had stayed previously. I planned to spend a week doing some photography out on the west coast, meet Marilyn on her arrival in Santiago and stay on at the cottage together for another week or so for her to recover a bit before heading home.

The whole plan worked like a dream. I enjoyed a week of solo photography; Marilyn walked the entire five hundred miles without any physical problems, had the time of her life and was totally hooked. I felt so incredibly proud of her.

It was fascinating while she was away for me to follow her route on the map. Most days I would receive a text message to say where she had been or would be spending the night. I then Googled the location and there suddenly my screen was full of maps, aerial views and any number of online images so that I could also see pretty much the same things as she was. Wonderful thing the internet. Some days I could tell from her tone that she had perhaps found it a bit hard or that a particular *hostal* had been a challenge *"with all the snoring and other unmentionable sound effects I had very little sleep"*

On other days I would get a message *"Tonight I am in heaven. Fed up with bad sleeping so treated myself to a pension. Single room with en-suite and balcony. Showered, slept, and now enjoying a glass of wine while I soak up the view before heading off to find some dinner."* Messages like that always gave me a lift.

ii

Returning from Spain and picking up the threads of normal life after ten weeks in such a different environment was a real challenge for Marilyn. But true to her word, Sherill the hotel manager had held the job which did help recreate some continuity for her. It was better than that because in her absence the hotel had been reorganising and the post of Assistant Manager created with Marilyn in mind. She could hardly refuse.

It was clear that the Camino had been a major influence on Marilyn and it seemed that she was scarcely home before she was talking about doing another one. Well, that wasn't going to be possible in 2010 because we had already planned a fairly major trip to Jordan that year as the ancient ruins at Petra had long been on our 'planned to visit' list.

However, from 2011 until 2017 inclusive Marilyn was out there walking one of the many Camino routes to Santiago at least once if not twice in a year. These included short routes like the Camino Ingles from Ferrol near La Coruña and the Finesterra route from Santiago to the coast.

To many people's surprise and curiosity, Marilyn had always preferred to walk alone. She enjoyed the casual acquaintances made along the way but when actually walking she likes the pleasure of that semi-meditative state where the route, the natural surroundings, the next step, and the next bed are the only things in mind.

Friends have asked her if she is afraid to which her answer is *"What of? All of life contains an element of risk so why would I believe that out along a path in the middle of nowhere there is an accident waiting to happen just for me or some person planning to do me harm. Yes, such things can happen but I could also fall under a bus at home. It's not worth thinking about"*

That said, I do recall there was one thing that worried her a little. She had read Bill Bryson's book 'A Walk in the Woods', which is his account of walking the Appalachian Trail where the risks include bear encounters. So when her pre-camino planning revealed that there are still bears in some of the Spanish mountains it did shake her confidence a tad, but not for long.

As a *'peregrino'* or pilgrim on the Camino, it is usual to stay in pilgrim *hostals* or *'albergues'* and it is in these places along the way that the walkers received stamps in the pilgrim passport – a kind of log book. This is inspected on arrival in Santiago to prove that an individual has indeed done the journey and is entitled to receive the *Compostela*, a beautiful document, hand-written in Latin confirming completion of the pilgrimage.

These *hostals* are often staffed by volunteers known as *'hospitaleros'* who are frequently former Camino walkers looking to give something back for the care and kindness they received whilst on the route. Marilyn became quite enthusiastic about doing this herself and then once again our old idea of having our own accommodation business in Spain resurfaced.

She was very keen on the idea but I was less so although not totally against it at that point. To research it a bit more we began to look again at properties in Galicia where ancient and characterful stone houses were both plentiful and ridiculously cheap, at least by UK standards. We targeted towns and villages along the route where according to Marilyn's knowledge there was a shortage of accommodation and we visited several and even got quite close to making an offer on one or two.

However, we didn't take that step because when the chips were down it was me whose courage failed and in retrospect, I am pleased we didn't. I think this was due in part to the fact of our previous negative experience in Catalunya; the considerable cost that would have been involved in creating something we could be really proud of and our knowledge of the difficulty of re-selling should we decide later not to continue. Also, I have to acknowledge that by this time being several years older I had rather lost my nerve for that level of risk and adventure.

We even discussed whether Marilyn might volunteer by herself as part of a team in a *hostal* run by someone else while I stayed home to keep things going here in the UK. We were both up for it in theory but one way or another it didn't happen. I've always felt a bit sorry, not to say guilty at having stifled Marilyn's sense of adventure but it was what it was and it's now history.

So finally now I guess, the idea of a long term life in Spain was confined to the 'unrealised daydream' box but our love for country, its people and culture are undiminished and I believe will ever be thus.

16 MORE PHOTOGRAPHY AND MUCH MORE TRAVEL

i

Following my compulsory, but frankly welcome, early retirement from the police I did have a police pension, and whilst it was very welcome, we still needed to work to continue doing the things we enjoyed. And work we certainly did in the variety of ways already described. I could say we have been lucky, which would be true, but I believe we have also made a certain amount of our luck too by careful thinking and planning. In any event, the result has been a varied and interesting life interspersed with a great deal of travel which we have both loved. I feel very blessed.

For us at home, life carried on pretty much as normal; jointly running the B&B; Marilyn working at the hotel and me still doing my various bits and pieces. Although by this time it was much less of the hands-on practical stuff and a great deal more of the estate agent copy-writing and private chauffeuring. I even added in another little driving job for the local Porsche garage in Ewhurst. I do like my sporty cars.

The fact that my state pension had arrived in 2009 made it easier to back off from the woodworking and do more of the other stuff which also included more and more photography. I did at least two more courses at West Dean College on various aspects of photography including landscape, studio lighting for portraiture and another in September 2009 that used the Goodwood Revival Meeting as its main area of interest. It was a clever piece of marketing by West Dean that utilised their proximity to the Goodwood motor racing circuit as included in the course fee was admission to the circuit on two days and entry to the paddock.

Well, with my interest in cars and motor racing this course was right up my street and provided scope to learn techniques for a couple of different types of photography. One was how to capture movement using either a panning technique or a very fast shutter speed. For a panning shot, the camera follows a moving car (or another object) to create a nice background blur giving the impression of speed whilst the fast shutter speed freezes all motion for maximum detail.

These minis racing really took me back to my first race meeting at Crystal Palace in the 60s

The other learning point on this course was how to make use of a telephoto lens to obtain candid shots of visitors and /or drivers who were mostly dressed in a variety of different styles harking back to the forties, fifties and sixties. Not having to ask permission provided anonymity and

the opportunity to capture some interesting and unguarded moments.

I think perhaps it was capturing these candid shots that really sowed the seed of interest in photographing people and I started to find portraiture, both candid and arranged, really fascinating.

I have continued to develop this style for street photography and it really is rewarding to capture life in 'candid' mode. Some might say it is intrusive but the law is very much on the side of photographers regarding people in public places. However, I would never in a million years seek to embarrass anyone unlike certain paparazzi photographers for whom intrusion seems to be the prime objective.

Although I love to see and am interested in wildlife, I have never been very bothered about photographing it. Simply don't have the patience I guess. Mind you, I have huge admiration for those who do and of course, their results do reward the effort. I am reminded of a member at the Cranleigh Camera Club who set himself up for hours to sit on a riverbank watching a hole on the other side. I've no idea how long it took him although he admitted it was some hours but eventually the water vole that he had previously seen pop into the burrow popped out again, picked up a blade of grass and preceded to happily eat it while Reg captured some of the most delightful small wildlife shots I've ever seen.

My efforts at something similar were a bit of a cheat really and courtesy of my sister-in-law Janice who gave me a ticket to a Photographers Day at the Surrey Wildlife Centre. On a day when the public is not admitted small groups of photographers were accompanied into the various enclosures by keepers carrying buckets of food mostly in the form of dead newly-hatched chicks from a nearby chicken farm. (I hasten to add that these were casualties and not deliberately killed.)

It was brilliant because we were able to be within a few feet of foxes and baby otters that were literally running over our feet. Birds of prey were brought out for us to snap and we were also able to look in on wildcats and badgers. It was quite unnatural of course and the animals were far too tame but I did come away with some superb images. Otters may well look cuddly, furry creatures but presented with a fish to deal with the 'red in tooth and claw' characteristics were immediately apparent.

.

ii

As 2009 drew to a close the south of England was treated to a white Christmas and the first in any part of the UK since 2004. The heavy snow came in from the east the previous week and caused the usual disruption to life as it always does here. It provided some lovely photographic opportunities though and I was still snapping away on 7th January.

Early 2010 saw our life continuing much the same really with the B&B as our main activity for additional income as well as a fairly steady stream of work from the estate agents which I continued to enjoy.

Our travel plans for this year were mostly arranged around a planned and fairly expensive trip to Jordan scheduled for September so we couldn't really afford anything else that was going to cost a lot although in February we did manage to get away to Dorset for a few days with our friends Jill and Clive. Only possible as our accommodation was a flat owned by another friend that we had at a very low cost. We walked and enjoyed some good pub meals and I of course had the camera so was happy.

In July, for my birthday we went to Paris for the day. Sounds extravagant I guess but thanks to a Eurotunnel day return it was easily managed and enormous fun and yet more interesting photographs descended onto my computer hard drive.

All very satisfying if you're a photographer but to be honest once I start with the camera Marilyn very quickly tunes out. It's fortunate that she still had her walking plans so a pattern began to emerge around each of us doing our own solo trips a couple of times a year and then joint ventures to places we both wanted to visit which was going to be precisely the case with the Jordan trip.

On the day after my birthday, I did receive a late birthday present as I was judged the overall winner of a photography competition at a local village fair.

Jordan happened in September and was a brilliant trip. Unusually for us, we had opted for an accompanied tour that included a local guide and nice hotels which made a change from our more accustomed DIY travel plans and cut-price accommodation.

The trip started in Amman where we visited the many and various Roman ruins including the amphitheatre, Citadel, Temple of Hercules and the fabulous ancient ruins at nearby Jerash with its hippodrome and Hadrian's triumphal arch. So spectacular, and as you might imagine I was in seventh heaven with the camera.

Hadrian's Arch in Jerash Jordan

From Amman, we moved via several interesting historic sites to Petra the ancient 'rose-red city' in the desert. The ancient site is approached through the 'siq', a deep and narrow water-carved defile at the end of which the vision of the 'Treasury' awaits.

This incredible edifice is carved from the red sandstone and has been dated to as early as five centuries BC. The site at Petra is vast and far too much to describe here but truly merits the description *'once seen – never forgotten'*. Everyone should go at some time in their life.

From the sophistication (albeit now in ruins) of Petra, we moved on to Wadi Rum. Known also as the Valley of the Moon, Wadi Rum is a valley cut into the sandstone and granite rock in southern Jordan 60 km to the east of Aqaba; it is the largest wadi in Jordan and was named a UNESCO World Heritage Site in 2011.

Wadi Rum has been inhabited by many cultures since prehistoric times, with several, including the Nabataeans, leaving their mark in the form of petroglyphs, inscriptions, and temple. In the west, Wadi Rum may be best known for its connection with British officer T. E. Lawrence, who passed through several times during the Arab Revolt of 1917–18. In the 1980s one of the rock formations in Wadi Rum, originally known as Jabal al-Mazmar (The Mountain of the Plague), was named "The Seven Pillars of Wisdom," after Lawrence's book penned in the aftermath of the war, though the 'Seven Pillars' referred to in the book have no connection with Rum.

The scale of the landscape with its looming and precipitous rocks and their red colour is my abiding impression along with the utter barren beauty of the place.

From Rum we headed for the Dead Sea where we were booked into the super-luxurious Ramada Resort. At almost four hundred metres below worldwide seal level the Dead Sea is the lowest place on the planet and on some occasions one of the hottest and driest too. Here predictably, we did the tourist thing, floating in the incredibly dense and salty water and watched as others plastered themselves in the black mud of the seashore – supposed to be a great skin treatment.

Our final destination en-route back to Amman was Qasr el Yahud, one of the most important sites for Christian pilgrims visiting the Holy Land and identified as the traditional site of Jesus' baptism. The place is located in the wilderness of the Jordan River Valley, north of the Dead Sea and east of Jericho.

This is me looking the intrepid photographer in Petra.

Although brought up as a catholic and raised on the Bible stories including those about John the Baptist, I no longer adhere to those beliefs. However, there was just something about the location that touched a spot inside and seemed to reach way back to those ancient times and tales that once meant a lot to me and left me feeling moved and deeply sad. Perhaps I subconsciously mourn my lost faith.

iii

We certainly didn't let the grass grow back in those days because within a month of our return from Jordan we were off again. This time it was back to our beloved Spain to have a bit of a road trip and visit some of the places Marilyn had been through whilst walking The Camino the previous year.

The plan had been to take our own car and drive down the western side of France and visit the Bordeaux region as we had never been there. However, a short time before we were due to leave, we learnt of a tanker driver strike in south-west France, as a result of which petrol stations were struggling to meet demand. To get around this problem we took the overnight car ferry from Portsmouth to Santander and by-passed the whole of France.

After a night in Santander, we drove east along the north coast towards Bilbao before turning south and then a short distance north into the Pyrenees and the small town of Roncesvalles.

Located quite high up in the mountains and just on the Spanish side of the border, this was where Marilyn had elected to start her Camino the year before. The more usual start point for this Camino route is at St Jean Pied de Porte on the French side of the Pyrenean range. However, as it was her first attempt at such a walk and owing to the shortage of accommodation on that first leg she decided to start just over the pass.

So this was where my brief introduction to the Camino began and where we stayed in the same pension as she had before setting out for her trek.

There was something quite special about the place both in respect of the air freshness at that altitude along with the light and the autumn colours that were just starting to really glow. We gave ourselves a short lie-in the following morning and as Marilyn explained she would have been on the road a couple of hours by the time we stirred. Nevertheless, when I looked from our window there was still a small stream of pilgrims emerging from the hostal and setting out with their backpacks and staves in hand for the walk down the mountain and on into Spain heading for Santiago some 790 kilometres away to the west.

After breakfast in the pension, we explored the village a little including the monastery where the monks run the *albergue* and have been providing shelter for pilgrims since the 12th century. The resident canons hold a Vespers service each evening and offer a blessing to pilgrims who will be setting off the next day. Although these days the Camino is less of a religious pilgrimage than in the past, I did sense a strong atmosphere of spirituality and brotherhood attaching to the whole place and the pilgrims we saw.

From Roncesvalles, we followed narrow country roads steeply downhill heading in the general direction of Pamplona. We passed through several villages where in most cases we saw small bars and cafes serving bottled water, coffee and general refreshment to pilgrims before eventually arriving at Zubiri which Marilyn explained had been her bed-stop on the first night of her journey.

Marilyn somewhere between Roncesvalles and Zubiri

We carried on the relatively short distance to Pamplona where we were to stay for a night. Pamplona is an attractive city and of course, rendered more interesting by its tradition of the St Fermin festival in July. The world-famous running of the bulls through the streets of the city was immortalised by author Ernest Hemingway in his 1926 book The Sun Also Rises following his visit there the previous year.

We had decided that after Pamplona we would head gently east along the foot of the mountain in the general direction of our flat in Catalunya but then I had another idea.

iv

Whilst we were in Roncesvalles, I remembered reading an article by Matthew Parris about a huge abandoned railway station in the Pyrenees and on looking it up again discovered that we were going to be passing quite nearby. I thought it sounded too good a photographic opportunity to miss. So, from Pamplona, we headed to Jaca and booked a couple of nights accommodation from where we could explore *Estacion Canfranc*.

The abandoned station at Canfranc

One of the old abandoned rail carriages at Canfranc

Rather than describing it from scratch and repeating research, I'm going to insert an article I later wrote about the Canfranc Station that was published along with my own photos in the Transport Trust Digest.

Canfranc Station

Faced with the need to punctuate a lengthy drive across the Iberian peninsular, I suddenly, and very happily as it turned out, remembered an article that I'd read about Canfranc Station and decided that this was an ideal opportunity to seek it out and perhaps get some interesting photographs.

Situated in a hidden valley flanked by verdant slopes and rocky crags near Jaca in the Western Pyrenees and some 4000 feet above sea level; this incredible granite and slate edifice is in the style of a French chateau. As long as the palace of Westminster it can best be described as the victory of national pride and hope over reality.

From as early as the mid-19th century the idea of a trans-Pyrenean rail link between France and Spain had been proposed and rejected on several occasions. Initially owing to the difficulty of the terrain and later because another route was already being built that followed the Basque coast and thereby avoided many of the obvious difficulties.

However, it seems that somewhere along the line the idea had been picked up at a high level in both countries and in particular had captured the imagination of King Alfonso XIII of Spain; who, it has to be said, was a man of some vision and even then, an enthusiastic promoter of tourism in Spain. It was he who instigated the Paradors, that wonderful chain of state-run hotels in historic and unusual places, but not before he had organised the building of the 400 room Hotel Palace in Madrid simply to accommodate his wedding guests. I guess it would have been hard to discourage such a man especially as he happened to be the King of Spain.

Certainly, by today's criteria, the project is unlikely to ever have got off the ground. Because, even disregarding the enormous technical difficulties, a cost-benefit analysis would undoubtedly have shown, as indeed proved to be the case, that the commercial potential was illusory. Adding into the equation the development of other simpler rail routes, improved and improving road networks it really should have been a 'no-brainer' even then, and obvious that the project was ill-advised to say the least.

However, naysayers notwithstanding, in 1904 a treaty between France and Spain was signed and work got underway. The challenges were formidable but I guess the truth is that without the imagination and sometimes-misplaced optimism of visionaries down the ages, frontiers in engineering and many other fields of endeavour would have advanced much less rapidly.

Long before work began on construction of the station building itself, railway routes had to be determined and then constructed. This alone required huge deforestation works and the construction of no less than eighty bridges, four viaducts and twenty-four tunnels. The longest of these was the five-mile stretch through solid rock that finally arrived from France into the hidden valley of the upper Aragon river that had been chosen as the site of the station building. Here, a mile of the river itself was re-routed and enormous earthworks carried out to protect the station area in the case of avalanche.

Created by Spanish architect Fernando Ramirez de Dampierre, construction of the station building lasted four years from 1921 until 1924, which at its completion was the largest station in Europe and at 750 feet in length, surpassed our own St Pancras.

This breath-taking three-storey Art Nouveau structure with three towers, one at each end and one in the centre, was long enough for three passenger trains and had no less than 75 doors along each side and more windows than days in the year. The building was finally opened in 1928 amid huge pomp and with the attendance of both the Spanish King and the French President Gaston Doumergue. From inception to completion Estacion Canfranc was the culmination of a 40-year project between the French and Spanish governments that was intended to provide the principal international rail terminal between the two countries.

The design was largely influenced by the fact that French and Spanish railways operated on different track gauges that prevented through traffic and necessitated a change of trains at the border. French trains entering the valley via the long tunnel arrived at one side of the huge terminal where passengers were welcomed in a vast vaulted customs hall with marble stairs, frescoed ceilings and mahogany counters. The building also included a huge area of administrative offices, a sumptuous hotel and even an infirmary. After a customs inspection and suitable refreshment or accommodation, passengers re-boarded on the other side of the terminal to continue their journeys into Spain.

In addition to the main terminal building there were extensive warehouse and workshop buildings and judging from the area between the buildings and the few remnants of track still in evidence there must have been a very extensive marshalling yard. However, even allowing for a huge level of over-optimism, national pride and plain old-fashioned misjudgement it is difficult to see how anyone could have envisaged the route generating sufficient traffic to justify a project on this scale.

Canfranc continued in operation for many years, even surviving the depression of the 1930s and the Second World War but the truth was that traffic never did reach the hoped-for levels due to the development of alternative coastal routes.

Sadly, the whole project came to an end in 1970 when, after an accident destroyed a bridge on the French side, a train ended up in the river, fortunately without loss of life.

One can imagine a huge collective sigh of relief that an excuse had been provided to cease operations. Despite the existence of a treaty between the two countries to continue the project, international services were abandoned together with the vast collection of buildings and even some rolling stock that have remained stationary for 40 years as they slowly crumble away to nothing. Interestingly, there is still a Spanish service to Canfranc that I plan to take one day. A little two-coach train runs up from Zaragoza twice a day and I imagine, knowing the area, that it would be a trip worth taking.

Prior to the construction of the station, there was no settlement here apart from the village of Canfranc a couple of miles down the mountain. However, the project resulted in the development of the quite substantial town of 'Canfranc Estacion' populated both by incomers and local migration from Canfranc village presumably for work. Today several adequate hotels and restaurants are catering for the few visitors who still come to marvel or mourn the phenomenon that is Canfranc.

The route over the Pyrenees above Canfranc was originally not much more than one of the pilgrim routes from France to Santiago de Compostela. Today it is a good road and passable most of the year permitting an interesting if somewhat tortuous drive to be made over from Tarbes to Jaca, Pamplona or Zaragoza

Now photography was the main purpose of my visit and although the principal buildings are fenced off, by way of a little judicious trespass I was able to gain access to some areas and managed to take a good selection of interesting and atmospheric shots. These included decaying carriages, abandoned workshops and even the old boiler house where the detritus of years still includes huge lumps of coal and curiously a very large number of empty wine bottles!

Some work was done a few years ago to ensure that the roof remained weatherproof and the recent erection of fencing around the main building and various notices around the place suggest plans are afoot to make some use of the site although not a lot appears to be happening. Frankly one wonders where on earth enough paying customers would come from whatever the attraction. Sad, but in today's climate, I guess that Canfranc Estacion is set to stand silent a bit longer yet.

UPDATE

There is a lot to be learned on-line about Canfranc but the most interesting element to me now is the declared intention to actually do something significant with the site. Ambitious plans are afoot to re-establish the Canfranc station as an operational international rail terminal along the lines of its original purpose and use including a five-star hotel.

oooOOOooo

Soon after arriving back from Spain, I was off again on another photography course at West Dean. The tutor was Stephen Walby, the Sussex photographer who had run the Goodwood course the previous year and it was good to see him again and get the benefit of his expertise. The outside sessions included Arundel with its lovely castle, Chichester and the coast down at West Wittering and so even more interesting images arrived in my now considerable portfolio.

December arrived with snow in the middle of the month and the opportunity for some more very seasonal photography, then Christmas came and went and that was another very full year done.

AUTHOR'S NOTE at the time of writing.

It is the end of September 2020 and I want to put in here a note about what is going on in our life right now.

Until a few days ago I had written virtually nothing of this memoir for months – totally blocked and pre-occupied by what has been happening around us.
In January we had the first news that some sort of previously unknown virus had emerged, initially in China but was by then gaining enough ground to become world-wide news. Manifesting as in some ways similar to an influenza infection it was initially referred to as 'coronavirus' which is actually a generic name for a whole raft of viruses that include the common cold and the regular versions of flu that appear each year. However, it soon became clear that this one, called COVID-19 was very different in that the lung infections it caused were far more virulent and it also impacted other organs to a greater or lesser extent depending on an individual's underlying health condition.

By February the media were reporting that we were facing a pandemic that was seriously life-threatening and for which there was no known cure or protective vaccine. Within a week or so a wave of panic buying was in full spate with the main item in demand being toilet paper. This was curious as neither diarrhoea nor stomach upset were known symptoms. I'm still trying to work out what was going on there. It actually became something of a joke with any number of amusing cartoons and jokes on the subject popping up in social media.

These few lighter moments were very welcome as the overall effect of the situation was the creation of a doom-laden atmosphere that was not enhanced when the government put the whole country under a lock-down that restricted movement away from home apart from for food shopping, very limited exercise or collecting medicines. It wasn't as if there was nothing else going on in the world because here in Europe, we were in the midst of the fraught Brexit negotiations. Meanwhile, the idiot Trump on the other side of the Atlantic was busy trying to pretend the virus didn't exist or that it might be remedied by dosing oneself with disinfectant. God help us – he's the most powerful man on the planet!

So, coming up to date, the lockdown worked well in combatting the spread of the virus but not before our intensive care units were virtually overrun, the NHS was near to meltdown and forty thousand people were dead in the UK alone.

The social and economic impact was nothing short of disastrous as all schools closed, businesses ground to a halt with millions of workers being furloughed (a word hardly anyone knew) at vast cost to the taxpayer and others worked from home where they could. By the end of this summer, infections were deemed to be low enough here and in some other countries for some relaxation of restrictions but in a matter of a few weeks the numbers kicked off again and as of today we are facing increasing constraints to movement and work.

Frantic research is going on all over the world in a race to find an effective vaccine although most of the informed scientists are playing down any early breakthroughs – all apart from Trump who is so terrified that the vast number of deaths in the US will adversely affect his election prospects next month so he is loudly proclaiming the imminent arrival of a vaccine against even his own scientific advisors.

History will no doubt have a much more comprehensive take on the 2020 pandemic but I wanted to pop a note in here to give a bit of an idea of what it had been like to live through this time. Hardly surprising then that my creative juices have been somewhat stifled. However, for the last few days, I have felt more motivated and will try to continue this story.

25/09/2020

17 SOME MORE INTERESTING PLACES

i

In January 2011, courtesy of Marilyn's friend Juliette we had a week or so away in Dorset where we stayed in her flat at Lyme Regis chilling out and exploring a little while naturally enough, I gathered a few more images of the Jurassic Coast. In February there was a photographers' day at the Brooklands motor museum at Weybridge where one of the now-retired Concordes is on display so I managed to get some nice shots of that with an early Classic Aston Martin which made an interesting juxtaposition. Two serious speed machines of their respective times.

March was the next decent trip when we set off for a long weekend in

Hamburg. This trip was sparked by my son's interest in model making and we had heard of the amazing model world that is Miniatur Wunderland.

Housed in one of the historic warehouse buildings of the old port the model has sections depicting many countries of the world and seeks to show their railway systems, an airport, seaport and dioramas depicting many different aspects of life, work and leisure. I don't know what the statistics were at the time we went but as of 2020, they are phenomenal.

The model now occupies some 24,000 square feet of space and includes 1,300 trains made up of over 10,000 carriages, over 100,000 moving vehicles, 500,000 lights, 130,000 trees, and 400,000 human figurines. Planning is also in progress for the construction of sections for Central America, the Caribbean, Asia, England, Africa and The Netherlands. The level of detail defies belief and one does need a couple of visits to fully do it justice.

Hamburg, although a hundred kilometres inland, is a major port city in northern Germany, and is connected to the North Sea by the majestic Elbe River. The city is crossed by hundreds of canals, and also contains large areas of parkland. Since the advent of containerisation, the nature of the port's cargo handling has changed dramatically. Whilst in former times most of the activity took place around the dense areas of canals and warehouses on the north side of the river, today the majority of goods go through the vast container handling operation that has grown on the opposite bank and has consequently left numerous warehouses redundant.

In recent time the old area has undergone significant rebirth with imaginative use being made the characterful old warehouse buildings as residential accommodation (see left), offices and cultural amenities such as art galleries, museums and concert venues. In one case the imaginative conversion has involved the construction of an ultra-modern multi-level glass structure on top of a historic red brick warehouse building. Known as the Elbphilharmonie concert hall, it is the showpiece of the city today.

2011 marked the one-hundredth anniversary of the original Elbe Tunnel. This intriguing structure is a twin-bore vehicle and pedestrian tunnel fully lined with cream ceramic tiles and with the unusual (today) feature of the vehicles being taken down into the tunnel by lifts.

The old Elbe Tunnel

With a capacity of 150,000 vehicles a day the new Elbe tunnel is a different thing altogether. Opened in 1975, the tunnel takes eight lanes of traffic in four bores a total distance of just over three kilometres. This was a fascinating trip for us both that also provided some very interesting photography.

ii

Marilyn had been saying that she wanted to head off to Spain again to walk a bit more of the Camino de Santiago and in her research had discovered that there are a number of quite short routes, one of which is the Camino Inglés.

The historic pilgrimage enjoyed widespread fame throughout medieval Europe. Land and sea alike were traversed by routes full of spirituality leading to Santiago de Compostela. The English Way or 'seafaring way' was packed with pilgrims from Scandinavia, Flanders, England, Scotland and Ireland on their way to destination ports such as Ribadeo, Viveiro, Ferrol and La Coruna on the Galician coast.

Blessed by an exceptionally strategic location, the latter two coastal enclaves are the starting points of the two alternate itineraries that make up the English Way. The La Coruna-Santiago route covers a distance of 74km, while the stretch linking Ferrol-Santiago is 118km long. (credit for this last paragraph is due to www.FollowtheCamino.com , one of the many web sites on the subject)

It was the Camino Inglés from Ferrol that Marilyn had chosen which was handy as I had wanted to do some coastal photography on the Costa da Morte, that dramatic, beautiful and navigationally dangerous coast we had been introduced to by Pablo's parents on our first visit to Galicia six years earlier.

So, in early May, leaving the B&B in Lynne's care once again, we set off together but with very separate itineraries. For Marilyn, it would be long days walking and sleeping in basic hostals, while for me it would be relaxing days exploring with the camera and nights in comfy hotels. Not a bad deal to my mind.

I already had some appreciation of the local maritime climate that gives this corner of Spain the label 'Costa Verde'. The downside is that it can be a bit wet on occasions but with the benefit (to my mind) of limiting tourism to true lovers of the scenery and natural environment and deterring the 'sun, sea and Sangria' (or lager) brigade.

The next week or so was delightful as I simply followed my nose down narrow lanes to pretty villages, tiny coves, long silver beaches, windy hilltops and several lighthouses on rocky headlands. I was in heaven.

I explored old churchyards, ruined farmhouses, dipped my toes in the crystal clean but distinctly chilly Atlantic while recording the whole in some beautiful photographs. At least I think they are. I was about to say I don't much care what other people think but that would be dishonest because I do. Well, a bit at least.

After a week or so I joined up with Marilyn and we went out to watch the sunset by the lighthouse at Finisterre. A very romantic moment I remember and a great example of how two people with divergent interests can make things work well with a bit of give and take.

Finesterre Sunset

iii

Most people of my generation from Surrey or Sussex will know of Climping; a tiny hamlet and beach a couple of miles to the west of Littlehampton. Climping is nothing to write home about because there is almost nothing there but it was where we usually headed when I was a kid and our parents fancied a trip to the seaside at little or no cost.

At the end of the small country lane, there was a field with a sea wall and beyond that a shingle beach with sand at low tide. The field was open and used as a car park by visitors like us and was perfect for the picnic with our little spirit stove for a full day's visit or even a quick trip on a summer evening (once we had a car reliable enough to climb Bury Hill without boiling over).

What we didn't know back then was that a short distance away was a very nice private hotel that back in those early family days we certainly could not have afforded. However, times and circumstances change and nowadays with a few pounds more to play with Bailiffscourt Hotel and Spa has become a favourite for a special occasion dinner or even a quick coffee.

Why am I mentioning this? Well, partly to strike a chord with readers who might remember Climping but more because this was where at the end of May, Marilyn and I had booked a 'dinner, bed and breakfast' date for our anniversary and I rather wanted to tell you about the place.

Nowadays Bailiffscourt is not cheap to stay in and certainly for us is very much a 'special occasions only' option. However, it is very nice and has a fascinating history. It looks for all the world like a centuries-old medieval manor but it is in effect a superb 'fake'. Not that this takes anything from the experience. The following clip is taken from the hotel's website and used because I couldn't describe it any better.

'With all the appearance of an ancient manor house, Bailiffscourt's best-kept secret is that until 1927 it didn't exist. It was designed for Lord Moyne, then Walter Guinness of the brewing family, by the antiquarian and architect, Amyas Phillips.

His brief was to recreate a house in the medieval style, which was favoured by Lord Moyne's wife Evelyn. Phillips searched the country for original stone, woodwork, doors, windows and fireplaces, bringing them all together at Climping to create the exquisite country house and park that we see today.

Throughout the 1930s, Bailiffscourt played host to the high society of the day until the death of Lady Moyne in 1939, and in 1948 it became a privately owned hotel and in 1993 Historic Sussex Hotels bought and lovingly restored Bailiffscourt.'

I mentioned that we sometimes use it as a coffee venue which I can thoroughly recommend. At nine or ten pounds for two coffees that may sound far from a good deal but there is more to it. For that price we get to sit for as long as we like in a sunny walled garden with views over adjoining countryside or depending on the season, we might be inside relaxing on an antique sofa in front of a roaring fire. And it's not just two coffees. For the price, we always have two cafetières (two because I have decaf) which always give two to three cups each plus a plate of delicious biscuits. So the price is for an experience that to my mind is worth every penny. (Please note I am not being paid to advertise this place but simply wanted to share the info.)

However, as a seaside experience, Climping has changed quite dramatically from the relaxed and cost-free place I've described above. Some years ago now, someone bought the field where we used to park (or perhaps they already owned it). Whichever, the owner saw the opportunity to turn it into a nice little earner by starting to charge for parking and in due course barriers and entry payment machines were installed. On the plus side, a basic café and proper toilet block were built. Given the fact that Climping had somehow been rediscovered and brought to the attention of more beach seekers, it was certainly a good thing for the local woodland which years ago was where we always went to spend a penny.

Its renaissance hasn't lasted though as the shop and toilets are now closed and looking very run down while the entry barriers and machines have been damaged and left open. Add to this the very significant damage done to the beach and sea defences by the heavy storms of recent years and the future for this particular 'Secret Sussex' location looks grim.

With the beach shingle swept away, the sea wall was soon undercut and collapsed as shown above.

Fortunately for Bailiffscourt though, it is far enough away from the actual beach and expensive enough to set it apart and presumably continue for the foreseeable future. Have a look here and judge for yourself. https://www.hshotels.co.uk/bailiffscourt

iv

In early June 2011 Marilyn was off yet again on another section of the Camino. Having met quite a few pilgrims along the route in 2009, some of whom had walked from various northern European countries, Marilyn's attention had turned to France and she was interested to go 'back up the trail' so to speak and have a look at that part of the route.

Situated some five hundred kilometres from the Spanish border, Le Puy-en-Velay is a town in the Haute-Loire region of south-central France. It is known for the green lentils grown in the area, and as a gateway to the Santiago de Compostela pilgrimage trail. (Chemin de St Jacques in French).

The 12th-century Romanesque Notre Dame Cathedral has frescoes and a cloister and it is from here that following a daily service of blessing, the pilgrims of old and today's perhaps more secular hikers set out for Santiago.

Despite her inclination to walk alone, within a few days of setting out from Le Puy Marilyn fell in step with Brigitte another solo walker from Paris. The limitation of both languages restricted idle chatter somewhat but somehow they made a connection and walked the whole route more or less together and continued over the next few years in two or three-week stages. That was the best part of eight hundred miles; from Le Puy to the Pyrenees and then over to Santiago in Galicia.

Meanwhile, I took my camera to Dungeness. No, it doesn't at first sight, seem as exciting as walking from France to Spain, but it suits me. Actually, there is a good bit more to the place than meets the eye. But what mostly meets the eye, at first sight at least, is the nuclear power station. To be fair, it's a bit hard to miss and most people seem to regard it as a huge blot on the landscape. Now I don't wish to be contrary, but I honestly don't see it that way. It is certainly big but in the context of the whole rather beautifully desolate area, it is not so huge and although it is just a couple of large rectangular blocks, I don't find it that unsightly.

I'm certainly not going to say I'm massively in favour of nuclear power because I'm not, although by a small margin it is better than burning fossil fuels for our power production with the attendant pollution that causes. But nuclear is certainly not without its problems regarding the environment. It produces climate warming heat and then there is the ultra-long-term issue of decommissioning and storage or disposal of the by-products and waste. To my mind the energy/environmental dilemma can only be solved by the use of renewables like solar, wind and tidal; all of which are freely available and don't contribute directly to warming or pollution. True, there are energy costs in the production processes required to build all these systems but these should reduce over time as more of our energy is derived from these same renewables.

There is of course another major contribution that we could all make to benefit our environment and significantly impact global warming and that is to reduce dramatically the amount of flying and driving around we all do. Well, that's certainly not going to happen any time soon and certainly not voluntarily so I guess we will do the best we can and just have to live with the consequences or at least our children will. I'd better stop at this point because I'm well off topic, and let's get back to a bit about Dungeness.

Situated on the Kent coast about mid-way between Hastings and Folkestone, Dungeness is a foreland or triangular peninsular made up mostly of shingle and presumably the result of the west to east longshore drift along the Channel coast. It is now one of the largest areas of shingle in Europe and provides a fantastic habitat for an extensive range of flora and fauna. As such it benefits from any number of ecological and environmental designations intended to protect it. There is an RSPB reserve there too which is highly regarded in ornithological circles and there is a plethora of online material available if you are interested.

The history of Dungeness is interesting. There have been seven lighthouses there over the years, five high and two low, with the fifth high one still fully operational today. In addition to the power station and lighthouse, there is a collection of dwellings. Most are wooden weatherboard beach houses, but there are also around 30 homes converted from old railway coaches in the 1920s. For generations, a vibrant beach-launched fishing fleet worked from Dungeness taking mostly herring but today the number of boats still operating is down to about four.

I've already confessed to my liking for a bit of rust and decay, so for me and the camera, the main attraction in addition to lovely wide seascapes was the detritus of the sadly vanished fishing fleet. This comes in the shape of rusty remains of winches, cabins and even the boats themselves left high and dry to fade away in the wind and rain.

For the next six months, we seemed to be on the move almost constantly. The first trip was to our friends in Spain for just a long weekend to join them for the San Joan celebration on 23rd June which is always a great party.

In August I headed off to Scotland for another photographic course run by a former West Midlands Police scenes of crime officer. Keith Hart had learnt his photography in the course of his time with the force and seen an opportunity to make use of his skills in retirement. Calling himself Photo4x4 he used his local knowledge and a 'go-anywhere' four-wheel-drive to get clients off the road to places they generally would not find. It was a cool idea and I got some lovely images as well as developing my skills with the aid of his lengthy expertise and experience. We drove miles together around the Highlands and you can imagine the chat that went on between a pair of old coppers. Great fun. After my few days with Keith, I headed off alone around the Highlands to put theory into practice.

Keith had a couple of interesting sidelines too. One was also to do with photography which involved him with the 'Round Britain' cruise ships that called into the Moray Firth. His role was to collect a few passengers who had opted for his photo-tour, doing a quick whizz round his well-rehearsed locations and deliver them back to the ship. From his point of view, with the trips being pre-booked on board by the clients at the beginning of the cruise, it was a great deal. If the weather turned foul on the day Keith still received his fee whether the clients decided to come or stay on board.

The oil jetty in Nigg Bay on Moray Firth

Following on swiftly from my solo Scottish trip was a joint foray into Germany where I had never been although Marilyn had visited a couple of times in her earlier travelling years. We took a chalet in Garmisch-Partenkirchen from where we explored extensively taking in several of the mad king Ludwig's Bavarian castles, pretty villages, impressive mountain scenery and a quick pop over the border to Innsbruck in Austria.

In October we went with friends Jill and Clive to Kraków which was very interesting. We rented a two-bedroom apartment in the city centre just a short walk from the main square. The idea of an apartment was to self-cater for breakfast at least, but to be honest the cafes in the town were so good and such excellent value that we didn't bother with more than a cup of tea before heading out for super breakfasts for the equivalent of about three pounds.

Not far from Kraków town is the Wieliczka Salt Mine which is definitely worth a visit. Visitors are taken down a couple of levels from where you can follow passages to different parts of the mine. There are the predictable static displays of figures showing how the salt was extracted in the confined spaces and so on but the real treat is The King's Chapel. Yes, a chapel. Actually, it is one of four and has to be seen to be believed.

There is loads of information on line about the mine but the following is an extract from the Wikipedia pages:

The mine is currently one of Poland's official historic monuments, whose attractions include dozens of statues and four chapels carved out of the rock salt by the miners. The older sculptures have been supplemented with new carvings made by contemporary artists. About 1.2 million people visit the Wieliczka Salt Mine annually

One of the chapels and a reception room is used for private functions, including weddings. A chamber has walls carved by miners to resemble wood, as in wooden churches built in early centuries. A wooden staircase provides access to the mine's 64-metre (210-foot) level. A 3-kilometre (1.9-mile) tour features corridors, chapels, statues, and an underground lake, 135 metres (443 ft) underground. A lift returns visitors to the surface taking about 30 seconds to make the trip.

Some of the carvings are quite outstanding in their skill and detail. For example, there is one depicting The Last Supper in which the perspective achieved is so remarkable considering that the depth of cut into the salt is little more than three inches or so. Even more amazing is that the miners who made it were not trained artists.

Image carved into the rock salt of the mine

Also, quite nearby to Kraków is the Auschwitz death camp now preserved and immortalized as a tribute to the many who lost their lives there. Having seen much about it on TV over the years I couldn't bring myself to visit although Jill and Clive did and found it a very moving and sobering experience.

18   MOROCCO FOR CHRISTMAS

My son Robert had spent a couple of months in Morocco during the summer and it was the description of his accommodation in Marrakech that had first prompted the idea of a Christmas opt-out. It sounded so perfect and the ideal opportunity to escape some of the seasonal hype and more or less obligatory over-indulgence. We had originally intended to go alone but when my sister also expressed an interest we jumped at the idea. Firstly, because she is great company and secondly because she speaks French.

We'd been there before a few years ago and stayed in a fairly up-market hotel outside the medina and as a result, an abiding memory had been running the gauntlet of the dozens of locals that used to tag along all the way from the hotel to the main square pestering to be our guide or show us the best bargains etc. etc. On one occasion I got so irritated that a guy told me "*You have a white face but a black heart*"

It's all about understanding the local culture really; the important part that bargaining plays in normal life and of course who can blame people who virtually live on the streets for trying to persuade unimaginably rich visitors to part with a little money. Once you can tune in to these and other aspects of Arab culture you should be able to chill a bit – at least that's the theory.

This time however we had booked to stay within the medina – the original old walled town, in a riad, a traditional Moroccan town house built around an internal patio.

For me, part of the excitement of independent (as opposed to tour operator) travelling is the doubt, however slight, that the carefully made arrangements will actually work. However, on this occasion our confidence was boosted by the arrival two days before departure of an e-mail from Gerard our host, confirming that his driver Rachid (who I kept wanting to call Radish) would meet us at the airport, and secondly as we were arriving late would we like him to prepare a light supper for us.

From this point on everything about the Riad, Gerard and his staff just got better notwithstanding momentary butterflies at the brand new and incredibly modern airport, when Rachid failed to appear. However, the flight was almost half an hour early so after a few tense moments and right on time, a smiling Rachid came breezing into arrivals. Twenty minutes or so later we disembarked from his slightly rattly minibus into a chaotic parking area where Rachid grabbed a couple of our wheelie bags and set off briskly, bidding us follow.

It certainly wasn't far but after a couple of turns through narrow dimly lit alleys of tiny shops selling everything from bread to sheep's heads and carpets to kerosene lamps, I felt quite lost, and I'm reckoned to have a good sense of direction.

Suddenly we had arrived and entered through a substantially studded door in the plain windowless ochre-coloured wall of the narrow alley. We found ourselves in a dimly lit and richly carpeted narrow hall and thence emerged via a short passage into a haven of tranquillity.

The first impression was the smell of frankincense born on wisps of smoke from small burners in the corners of the central patio. This was an area some 40 or 50 square metres lit by numerous flickering candles, their perforated metal lanterns casting magical patterns of light across the walls and floor. The entire area was superbly tiled, diagonally and quite plainly across the floor and then for about four feet up the walls with richly patterned coloured tiles that echoed those surrounding the small fountain in the centre where water trickled gently. In each corner was a small tree, two bananas and two oranges whilst in the background, we could hear the gentle strains of the music from Swan Lake. The name of the riad was Dar Limoun Amara. – "House of the red orange".

Marilyn and Angela taking in their surroundings.

Within a moment or two, a good-looking middle-aged man emerged smiling from a side room. *"Hello, I'm Gerard Barbier."* he said, and coming immediately to greet us he offered a strong and noticeably well-manicured hand.

He had a pleasantly firm grip but I noticed his skin was softer than I'd expected that suggested someone else was doing the housework. Though not especially quiet, his voice had a kind of 'soft around the edges' quality with that enviable (but infuriating if you don't have it), French accent that makes women go weak at the knees.

Adopting the perfect host mode, Gerard immediately offered a drink, tea, juice, or wine if we wanted, and enquired about our journey, remarking on how early the flight was before leaving briefly to pass our order to as yet unseen helpers who could nevertheless be heard elsewhere in the building.

Waiting for the drink we chatted as Gerard showed us around the ground floor that comprised the central patio with guest rooms on two of the sides, and a sitting room with TV and internet access and a small breakfast room on the other sides. A passage to the kitchen led off from one corner while the stairs to the first floor were in another.

I put Gerard at around fifty or so, quite tall and broad-shouldered with an open, tanned face, sparkly brown eyes and very fair or maybe silver hair, cut short and swept back. He was casually dressed in jeans and navy-blue jumper. Leading the way up the stairs, Gerard said *"Let's show you the rooms. After that, we have some supper for you."*

We had two rooms, both on the first floor and leading off a balcony that ran around three sides of the patio well. The rooms were charming; simply but traditionally furnished in Moroccan style with brightly coloured tiles, carved wooden screens and painted furniture.

We were all quite hungry so without unpacking, we went back down for the food where a table had been laid up in the side room and a small oil-filled radiator was being remarkably successful in lifting the chill a few degrees.

Once seated in the cosy dining room Gerard explained what he had arranged for supper. *"You said you wouldn't want much so we have made soup and some salad. The soup is called harira and it's made with fresh tomatoes and lentils but it's flavoured with a variety of herbs and spices. It's one of my favourites especially when it's a bit cold like now.*
Then there is some Moroccan salad. This one is a bit like a Greek salad with tomato, pepper, avocado and some cheese. Sounds a bit ordinary but Rachid makes a marvellous dressing."

Gerard also offered some Moroccan wine if we would like to try it. This was a surprise because being an Islamic state where the consumption of alcohol is strictly speaking forbidden, I hadn't expected to find any so openly available.

Gerard explained, *"It's not cheap, although it's cheaper than imported wine but not so good. See what you think. Muslims aren't supposed to drink alcohol but if you're not Muslim while it's not encouraged it's not prohibited."*

I had to smile at the pragmatic approach exhibited by the production of wine commercially to supply the boozy infidels. Gerard went off to fetch the wine and Hassan appeared with a basket of lovely warm bread closely followed by a tureen of the aromatic Harira.

Hassan, an older local man of around 60 was the sometimes waiter, porter, handyman and general factotum of the riad. Slightly built and shorter than Gerard; Hassan, who spoke only French and Arabic, was calm and very smiley with dark olive skin and black wavy hair.

After a couple of minutes, Gerard re-appeared with the wine and sat with us as we tucked in, explaining in response to our enquiry, a little about the riad and how he came to be in Marrakech.

"I'm from Bordeaux but my family always came to Morocco on holidays. I think a few generations back my family had some role in the old colonial days so it was rather in our blood and over time it's become a kind of second home. I still go back to Bordeaux a couple of times a year to get a break from the chaos here but I'm always pleased to get back."

I asked, *"Did you just turn up here one day and decide to run a riad."*

"Mon Dieu!" he laughed, slipping momentarily into French. *"That would have been crazy and impossible. Things don't work like that here. I started out in engineering in France but after a year or two, it didn't seem to fit me so I went and trained as a hairdresser, did what you would call an apprenticeship and then decided to go travelling around America working wherever I could – mostly it was illegal.*

I was away a couple of years, had a lot of experience and worked in some very classy places but when I got back to France I couldn't settle and decided to come down here. I worked as a waiter for a while and then was lucky to get a hairdressing job at The Mamounia Hotel. It was wonderful, so luxurious, even the staff rooms were good, not big, but very comfortable."

Hassan cleared away the Harira then came back with more bread and a plate of delicious-looking salad, finely chopped and with the most delicious dressing. Gerard poured some more wine, which was going down quite well by now. *"So how,"* asked Angela, *"did find your way from the Mamounia to here?"*

Gerard went on, *"I was very lucky. At the hotel I met a lot of famous and influential people and after a few years there when I was getting a bit bored, someone got me a job with Moroccan TV – still hairdressing but in a very different world. Much more exciting and demanding in many ways and so interesting but although I enjoyed it for quite a long time, even that became a bit routine so I left and went back to France for a while to see my family. Marrakech kept calling me back though so I came and got a job as a restaurant manager. I don't know quite how I managed to get it but that worked very well for a while and gave me an insight into another aspect of the hospitality world – not exactly The Mamounia but interesting."*

"I think the next thing that happened was that I got to know someone who was running a riad and then incredibly I heard that this one was for sale. Fortunately, but unlike a lot of those for sale, this one had had the renovation done and was already trading and to cut a very long story short I bought it four years ago and here we are."

My sister Angela used to own a restaurant and as we ran a B&B, we were all interested in the day-to-day operation of the riad and asked Gerard about it. He explained that he had a staff of three; Hassan who we'd already met, Rachida, his very able cook and Fatima who worked as housemaid and did all the rooms and that they had all been there when he took over the business.

After a leisurely meal, the effects of the long day travelling and the wine sent us off to our beds relatively early with the promise from Gerard to walk us into the centre in the morning and show us around a little.

Of course, you can never be sure of beds. Fortunately, these were fine and in no time at all it seemed; we'd slept and woken, and suitably refreshed were heading downstairs again to try out breakfast, which did not disappoint. Fresh fruit, yoghurt, two varieties of freshly made pancakes, the same delicious bread, home-made preserves, juice and tea or coffee were all on offer each day. More than enough to set us up for exploring what was to prove an interesting holiday.

True to his word, after breakfast Gerard escorted us on the ten minute or so walk from the riad to the main square (actually L shaped), Jemaa el Fnaa, the world-famous centre of Marrakech. Very kindly en-route he pointed out and recommended several restaurants as well as a couple to avoid.

And then we were on our own and immediately headed for the Café de France for coffee whilst we sat for half an hour or so watching the daily bustle of both local and tourist life pass before our eyes. This side of the square is actually a thoroughfare. I guess one could say "It's a road but not as we know it." Our seats were less than three metres away from the throng and separated only by a row of planters occupied by some seriously tired plants of what were probably of the Geranium family but once again, not as we knew it.

We soon discovered that the trick is not to catch the eye of any of the itinerant traders because once eye contact is made, they are over the planters in a flash with their cigarettes, shoelaces, pirated CD's, bottles of Argan oil or their boxes of shoe-shine gear.

Interestingly, there were relatively few cars, in fact it would have been virtually impossible to get a car through as the throng of humanity was so dense and seemed to flow in waves first one way and then the other. What there were though were dozens of bicycles and mopeds ridden by young and old alike who all seemed remarkably adept at weaving at speed between the crowds. In all the time we were there I only ever saw one near miss.

Brightly painted horse-drawn carriages called caleches also plied to and fro through the crowds invariably occupied by tourists, cameras in hand, happily snapping away apparently randomly in all directions.

The absence of motor traffic meant that noise levels were surprisingly low compared to home although there was of course a general background clamour punctuated by frequent moped horns or cycle bells and vendors calling their wares.

If I can recall a smell it would be of dust, strong coffee and spices with an overtone of horse manure that became almost unbearably acrid the closer one ventured to the main caleche parking area.

During the day the only stalls allowed in the square are a couple of dozen juice bars. These are ornately decorated trailers stacked high with brightly coloured oranges from where the vendors call out to every passer-by offering wonderfully sweet freshly squeezed orange and grapefruit juice.

Towards the centre of Jemaa el Fnaa away from the river of life that flows along the edges the scene changes. There are slightly fewer people and they seem less directed, being content to wander and take in the atmosphere and the sights.

In addition to visitors, there are of course the traders including the henna artists that I remembered from our last visit. Gerard had advised caution as some of them can be quite forceful and if you show the slightest interest will take your hand and, in a moment, you can find yourself painted whether you want it not. Even worse is the fact that some of the artists add chemicals to their dyes that can be an irritant to sensitive skin.

Then there are the water sellers in their bright red decorated cloaks and conical sequinned hats carrying their brass drinking cups and goatskin water containers as they wander the square ringing handbells to announce their service. Small and large groups of local people gather around storytellers, snake charmers and even scribes who sit on the ground waiting to read or write for clients.

There are of course vendors who sit beside the usual displays of tourist tat including everything from stuffed felt camels to useless brass ornaments and bottles of Argan oil and just about anything else you can't imagine wanting in a million years.

These four old chaps always seemed to be on this same seat watching the world go by, but don't remember seeing them actually talking.

It seems that all levels of local life are represented right down to small children trying to sell a few pastries and beggars who according to Gerard are for the most part genuinely destitute. Islam requires its adherents to make charitable donations and he told us that each area has its own population of down-and-outs who are supported by local residents.

Lunchtime was our – well my - first mistake, when we headed for a restaurant recommended by Gerard and I opted for another bowl of the delicious Harira which on this occasion turned out to taste slightly different which I just assumed was down to a different chef. The girls had something different and by late afternoon I knew they had made the right choice. I felt awful – that dreadful feeling of nausea that is somehow worse than being physically sick.

A sleepless night followed by a day in bed was not the ideal start. Gerard, true to his kindly nature went off and fetched some jollop from the pharmacy which helped a bit but basically, I had to just wait it out and by the following morning was feeling better – not brilliant but well enough I felt to resume being a tourist and so after, in my case, a very light breakfast, we set off again.

We had decided to head for the Mamounia Hotel, a 5-star paradise beloved of Winston Churchill and located within fabulous gardens just ten minutes or so from the bustle of Jemaa el Fnaa.

I was feeling better by now and so was rather involved in trying to get some decent photos and hadn't noticed that the girls had got some distance ahead so when I did, I picked up my pace to catch them up and in doing so I had to pass a row of parked caleches – the afore-mentioned horse-drawn carriages much used for ferrying tourists around the city.

Now, these horses are pretty-well bomb-proof so the fact that I'd have to walk through a fairly narrow gap between them and a parked car didn't give me a second thought. However, you know how it is sometimes when in that fleeting instant before something occurs you just know it, and I sensed as I came abreast of the horse that it was not going to be good but of course it was too late as everything seemed to go into slow motion.

It didn't really of course because quick as a flash the horse's head came round and it grabbed hold of my upper arm and just hung on. This was no little nip. I'd never experienced pain like it and the damn thing didn't want to let go or so it seemed.

After what must of course have been only a few seconds I managed to wrench my arm out of its grip and ran a few steps away when my legs just gave way and I collapsed on the pavement. I suppose it was shock and the pain, which was quite incredible.

Fortunately, and by complete chance, the girls had looked around to see me on the floor and came running back. *"The bloody horse bit me."* I shouted and then almost immediately passed out.

It was clear to the hotel staff there that something was wrong and they couldn't do enough, offering doctors or a car to hospital and so on. However, we went and sat on the terrace ordered some sweet tea and after a while I began to feel better as I contemplated that despite the pain, I'd been very lucky, because had I not been wearing a fleece the horse would certainly have taken a piece out of my arm. It did take me an hour or so to steady up and of course, my arm was almost black from shoulder to elbow within a couple of days but as I said, because of the fleece the horse's teeth didn't touch me and although the skin was broken there was no real risk of infection.

On Christmas Day we weren't allowed to forget the occasion completely as Gerard had arranged an extra special celebratory dinner for us. Certainly not with any seasonal fare we recognised but a most delicious series of courses that Gerard explained were reserved for special occasions in Moroccan culture.

For Angela's benefit, we made return visits to the Marjorelle or Yves St Laurent Gardens and then went with Rachid in the Riad mini-bus up the Ourika valley both of which I've mentioned previously in the book.

All in all, our Marrakech Riad was a great success and nicely diverted us from all thoughts of a traditional English Christmas although in a couple of days we back here in the aftermath and the wretched sales that had already begun. A very worthwhile exercise though and one we were destined to repeat a few years later although in a different part of the country.

Two local women in the Ourika valley processing Argan nuts to extract the oil which is used for a variety of purposes both cosmetic and medicinal.

19 ANOTHER NEW YEAR

So, January 2012 found us still in Peaslake and there was not a lot wrong with that I must say. The Garden Room was quiet of course, being the low season for tourism but we did still have the odd business client in for two or three nights at a time. Similarly, the early part of the year was quiet in the property market so I had relatively few properties to write up for Savills.

However, although I had stopped advertising my handyman activity by this time, work continued to come in from word-of-mouth referrals so that kept me fairly active and together with the occasional driving I was really as occupied as I wanted to be. This meant that I was able to devote most of my spare time to my developing photographic activity and memoir writing. Although I had started the writing around 2007/8 and attended the writing group for a couple of years, it was still the writing that seemed to get pushed to one side for lengthy periods by the camera.

It was probably around this time that I joined a local camera club; a group of enthusiastic folks that got together weekly to further our common interest. To that end, the organisers used to arrange visiting speakers to come and talk on their specific areas of interest or expertise and these were of course invariably illustrated with some stunning (and on occasions quite mediocre) examples of their work.

Another club activity was the competition programme in which some of my landscapes did quite well. Judging was by invited photographers acknowledged as experts in their craft although it must be said that some were less than impressive as judges and often talked more about themselves than about the images they had come to consider.

Another thing I found at the club and a couple of others I have tried over the years was that the members were a bit staid and not very adventurous in their work. I mean, there was a lot of absolutely superb landscape, wildlife, flowers, still life and so on but very little that was adventurous or challenging. There was one member called Peter who was very good at portraiture. His images were often very imaginative in concept and sometimes included more risqué styles like boudoir and artistic nude images but the reaction of many members seemed to be that this was not 'appropriate' material for their club. Personally, I loved the work; not for any prurient interest but for its originality, skill of technical execution, the beauty of the images and it must be said for the fact that he was pushing the club boundaries a bit which I felt was needed.

As a result of seeing his work, I started to take an interest in people photography but as none of my family was interested or near enough to act as models for me, I was a bit stuck for subject material.

I had no idea how to find or manage a shoot with a model even if I knew one so I asked Pete for help.

He very kindly agreed to arrange a joint shoot with a model he knew called Ellie with the express purpose of introducing me to her and the way a model shoot works. We had a great couple of hours at the atmospheric Waverley Abbey ruins near Farnham. To my delight, Ellie was both beautiful and totally normal with no diva-like pretensions.

We had a laugh, she climbed about on the ruins, Pete gave me appropriate guidance and I came away with some nice pictures that I am still very proud of.

On the travel front, we did less this year than last as the Moroccan trip had rather depleted the funds, however, we did manage a few 'away-days'.

Alex, the young Spanish boy we had taken into our home as a thirteen-year-old student back in the mid-'80s had by now followed in his father's footsteps and was a doctor himself. In 2006 we had been to his wedding to Aintzane, a charming girl from Bilbao, and also a doctor. As they had set up home close to Bilbao, we decided to combine a trip to see them with the opportunity to visit the city with its iconic Guggenheim Museum building. At the time of writing Alex is now a consultant in ophthalmology and like his father spends quite a bit of time visiting foreign parts, networking and delivering learned papers to peers and colleagues.

In May it was Spain yet again but this time to Galicia. The object was to catch up with Anna and Lluis whose basketry and weaving enterprise seemed to be going from strength to strength. We were thrilled to hear they were enjoying continuing success and were now a sought-after centre for universities to send students as interns. This was great for Anna as it allowed her to give the students weaving tasks whilst she was able to push on with design projects. For the latest on their activity and to check out some beautiful gifts have a look at www.annachampeney.com

While in that corner of the country we arranged to meet friends Juan and Cristina from La Coruña. These were Pablo's parents, another of the students who came to stay with us previously. We enjoyed several days touring with them and taking advantage of their local knowledge to show us places of interest while we stayed at several pazos. Now if you don't know about pazos, you should if you are ever in that corner of Spain.

Pazo (pronounced patho) is the Galician word for a manor or large country house and many have been converted to use for rural tourism. Not unlike the Paradors of Spain but usually smaller, the pazos are invariably old, historic and beautiful, featuring granite structures with steps and balustrades of carved granite around balconies whilst inside polished chestnut floors and joinery along with large stone fireplaces complete the ambience. And, they are not expensive for the standard of accommodation provided. The website is www.pazosdegalicia.com and very much worth a visit.

We also managed two short visits to our flat on the Costa Brava which was lovely. Marilyn completed another couple of weeks of the Camino through France towards the Pyrenees while I looked after the B&B and went out days from home with the camera. What do they say "Not a bad life if you don't weaken"? We were very fortunate and knew it.

20   THE BOOK GETS GOING AGAIN

i

I'm not quite sure why but in the spring of 2013 the unfinished book came back to my mind. Perhaps it was because I had pointed my camera at pretty much all the lovely Surrey landscapes within reach and needed a change. In any event, I resolved to really work at turning my bundle of notes and a few completed chapters into a finished and bound volume for which of course I would need some sort of publication and/or printing process. I had been encouraged by the writing group to try to get the thing published but none had any clear idea of how to turn the ambition into reality so it was for me to discover.

The first thing, however, was to actually finish the manuscript and then as a friend advised, edit and then edit again and again so I set to in earnest and eventually after several more months of part-time work felt it was ready for the next stage.

Writing and fine-tuning the work had been difficult enough but publication is a whole other issue. It soon became clear that in today's world when home technology can turn anyone into a photographer or writer, professional publishers are awash with submitted manuscripts from 'wannabe' JK Rowlings and can afford to be incredibly selective.

It seemed obvious to me that the life of 'an ordinary Joe' was unlikely to capture the imagination of a professional publisher and I was within a whisker of giving up on the idea of holding my own bound volume when I discovered self-publishing or 'vanity publishing' as it is sometimes unkindly (but often correctly) described.

The digital world has brought us 'print-on-demand' technology which means that any writer can pay and get a single copy of a book professionally produced for under a fiver. I learnt that many companies are offering this service with various levels of sophistication and support so I went for it. Initially, I decided to call the book 'Born in 44' because I felt that said it all. It was about the life of a person born in that year so to me that was an obvious title.

The first self-publishing company I used offered relatively little support or advice and whilst it was satisfying to hold that nicely bound volume the interior was disappointing in terms of font, layout, format and even paper quality. It was, however, probably at this point that I started to wonder if it might be worth doing the whole self-publishing thing, getting an ISBN and putting the book out there on Amazon and similar platforms just to see if anyone else might want to read it.

Dave and Eve Gary, the couple we had met in Spain have a friend who is a publisher although she doesn't deal with biography or memoir as a genre. She did however kindly agree to run her eye over that first volume and offered some very useful advice.

Apart from advising me to work harder on the interior layout like format, font, spacing etc., she told me the title was wrong. She felt it needed to be more specific to appeal to a more definable readership saying *"Everyone born in 1944 is a very large market but how are you going to reach them?"*

She suggested that I focus on something more specific like the location the story is set in and so the title became "Stepping Out from Ashtead" because it says everything about the content. Ashtead because that's where it is mostly set and 'stepping out' because that is precisely what is described – my journey from childhood and out into the wide world. And in terms of marketing, it gave a target readership that could be interested and was more easily identifiable.

The next company I found was an Amazon subsidiary called Create Space which is now Kindle Direct Publishing. Their set-up was (and is) much more comprehensive up to and including total hand-holding if required along the road to publication. However, their benefit to me was that they offered a template that included all the correctly dimensioned formatting so that the finished article would look good regardless of content. There was help along the way with the inclusion of pictures, the allocation of ISBNs, cover design, cover finish and final printing and the biggest benefit was that being part of the Amazon empire the book would be immediately available to a worldwide market.

The amazing thing was that it was free to download their 'desktop' with all the above-mentioned tools right up to the point where you are required to buy the first 'proof' copy to check over before authorizing further printing. So in 2015, the first Edition of Stepping Out from Ashtead went on sale and met with moderate success. I reviewed the content over the next few months and in 2017 published the second (and current) edition with some additions and amendments and I'm pleased to say that it is still selling. Not in any big way. It's not that sort of book, but pretty much every month I receive a small to medium royalty payment from Amazon.

What you don't get from Amazon/Kindle is any marketing assistance, or at least not without paying. So my marketing has been pretty lukewarm if I'm honest because the commercial motive never has been high on the agenda. I have made use of my Facebook page and various Facebook special interest groups with a connection to Ashtead and the surrounding area. Several groups focus on the nostalgia of the period the book covers, like the '40s, '50s and '60s. I also have a photographic web page with a blog section that I have been using to publish extracts from the book to generate a bit of interest; a ploy that seems to have worked quite well. I also managed to persuade a local free magazine from the Ashtead area to publish a little review of the book.

The reason why finishing the book took so long was that apart from whatever work I was doing, other interests waxed and waned along the way. One of these was genealogy. In the process of writing that first book, I wanted to talk a bit about my parents' backgrounds so as a first step I Googled mum's maiden name which was Hurson. The main thing this came up with was a Facebook hit on a group called The Hurson Grapevine. I was intrigued. It turned out that this group was run by one of my Irish cousins to keep the numerous members of the Hurson clan in touch; some of whom are distributed quite widely around the world.

This was a fantastic discovery for me as it brought me in touch with my cousins of which there are many and involved several trips to the Emerald Isle to meet and catch up with family I hadn't seen for some fifty years.

The genealogy also helped to clarify something about the origin of the Hurson name. Mum had often said she was "*descended from French nobility*", a claim that had never been verified one way or the other and she hadn't ever explained its basis. I was not adept enough at ploughing through genealogical records but we knew someone who was.

One of Marilyn's cousins was pretty much addicted to this sort of thing and jumped at the chance to have a look at it for us. There was a problem with the Irish records because a lot were destroyed at some point in a fire. Nevertheless, the outcome was interesting and persuasive if not exactly definitive.

Mum came originally from the Tyrone area of Northern Ireland where there are some suggestions of a historic French connection. There is a village called Husson in north-west France and it is a historical fact that when the Protestant Huguenots there were persecuted and driven out of France in the 17th century, many came to Ireland. Another theory suggested was that the ancestor may have been a mercenary soldier who arrived in Ireland to fight at the Battle of the Boyne in 1690. Thirdly, there are also some words in common use in the Tyrone area that share a French vernacular origin.

So, could this distant ancestor have been such an in-comer and known perhaps as *William of Husson* (not a real name – just me theorizing)? Soldiers have often fallen for local girls and stayed on in locations all around the globe. Could this have been the origin of the Hurson name? Far from conclusive and whilst hardly 'French nobility' as Mum might have imagined; I wonder how she would have reacted to this theory. – *"Descended from Protestants! I don't believe it."*

The genealogy became quite absorbing as a new interest and it was fascinating identifying historic information about Dad's side of the family too. I have identified a male ancestor George Simmons in West Horsley, Surrey as far back as the late 1700s and could probably do more if I went out to find parish records and cemeteries etc. Sadly, there is no nobility or hidden fortune on that side of the family either. They have all been farmworkers or similar until my grandparents who were coachman/chauffeur and housekeeper. It's definitely an interest I will continue with though.

Overall, the writing experience was very positive, providing good mental exercise and research skills, enjoyable in the actual practice, an interesting and useful development of my word-processing skills plus of course a handy, albeit small financial reward. As a result, I decided it would continue and the next memoir would be my police years.

ii

Talking about the book has taken us forward three or four years but there were one or two other milestones of note in 2013.

In May, Marilyn headed off again to meet Brigitte in France where they walked another hundred or so miles of the French Camino route from Moissac to Aire Sur L'Adur when I think they had the wettest walk she had yet experienced. She brought back photos of rivers in full spate, wet clothes and boots caked in mud and declared it had *"been great"*. Can't say it sounded that great to me although to be fair there were a lot of photos of some lovely convivial meals with lots of wine flowing which I guess was some consolation for the weather.

Reconnecting with my Irish relatives was a real bonus arising out of my family research. I learnt from my cousin Monica who more or less runs the Hurson Grapevine group that they try to have a reunion each year and I was invited to attend in July 2013. I was all set to go alone as Marilyn had always had a slightly negative attitude to Ireland due to its reputation for wet weather so I was delighted when she said she would like to come along and then to my greater surprise my daughter Maria did too.

I had intended to combine the visit to the relatives with a photographic tour of the south and I stuck with this plan although Marilyn drew the line at following me and the camera on a two-week stop-start photo tour.

Having enjoyed a great lunch and get-together with cousins I hadn't seen for many years, the following day I dropped the girls at the airport and set off on the road to my first stop at Bray.

This is a resort just south of Dublin where I had been once before as a child with my parents to visit my uncle Jimmy who had a guest house there. Pulling up in the town I found the location – no longer a guest house, but after calling into a couple of shops I soon managed to find someone who while not old enough to remember my uncle knew someone who probably would. A few minutes later I found myself in a jeweller's shop where the very elderly owner clearly remembered The Wicklow Hills guest house and my uncle too. (Along with his reputation for liking a drop of the hard stuff)

Although I only ever met Jimmy once I do have reason to be grateful to him as following his death my sister and I shared a small inheritance that would have been for my mother had she still been living. We had always understood that Jimmy had no family, but the big story to come out of reconnection with my cousins was that while he had never married, he did have a daughter – my cousin Gail.

Apparently, he had fathered a daughter out of wedlock and given social and religious attitudes to illegitimate births, the child had been given up for adoption. However, in later years she had decided to seek out her family and got in touch with my cousins near to where she lived in Dublin. Due to the persisting attitudes around illegitimacy, her existence was not immediately broadcast and sadly Jimmy died before he and his daughter could meet.

My next stop about half an hour along the road was the town of Arklow, where another uncle had lived. My namesake, Brian Hurson was a chemist and optician and had a business for many years in the town. I had stayed there for a couple of nights with him many years ago when camping in Ireland with the scouts.

I recognised the shop immediately although no longer a chemist's. I wondered if I might be as lucky here in finding someone who had known him so I wandered into the nearby pub and started a casual chat with another customer along the lines that my uncle used to have a chemist shop there. I struck lucky again and had found not one but on this occasion two people who had known him. They were all over me and telling other people in the pub who I was and *"Here let me get you a drink."* etc. It was really lovely, especially to hear the way he was so well regarded.

After Arklow, I continued my journey via Waterford and Cork, the Dingle peninsular and up the coast road the Irish Tourist people now market as The Wild Atlantic Way. It is certainly a wild coast with loads of wonderful photo opportunities that I made great use of, eventually flying back home from Shannon airport.

I resolved to return soon to get a look at the wild Donegal corner and then visit another set of cousins in the north.

iii

On the home and photographic front, things were going quite OK. The greetings cards I made were selling well in the local outlets and the Guildford Tourist Office and in August I had been asked to do the photography for the Peaslake village fair. Not as a paid commission of course, these sorts of things never are but you never really know what the spin-offs might be.

Anyway, it was great fun and I added quite a few images to my own collection. I had also been asked to do a portrait session for a neighbour and her husband that went very well and I enjoyed it enormously - another first.

In September 2013 Marilyn went with her friend Juliette to walk the short Camino route that starts from Santiago and goes to the lighthouse at Cape Finesterre or *Fisterra* in Gallego.

Meanwhile, I bit the bullet and joined an online model/photographer liaison group and arranged a photoshoot with a hobbyist model from Leatherhead. Emmeline was twenty-one, six feet tall, stunningly attractive, and like so many other girls I was to meet, was dabbling in a bit of modelling just for fun. With no great aspirations to be the world's next top model; she worked in an office in her father's company, played the drums in a band and enjoyed modelling for the experience and the confidence boost it gave her.

The arrangement between models like Emmeline and hobby photographers like me is known as TFP. This stands for 'time for prints' meaning the model gives her time free of charge in exchange for some images for her portfolio (not usually prints these days but digital images). The photographer gains practice and experience and no one has to pay anything. As the meerkat says, *"simples"*.

I was really beginning to develop a taste for people photography and was trying to work out how I could do more. As I didn't (and still don't) have the money to pay professional model rates it looked like I would have to stick with the TFP route. I have since completed many shoots and all have been on the exchange basis so I certainly cannot complain.

Here I would like to take the opportunity to dispel the notion held by many that the young women who go in for modelling are either air-heads with no serious attitude to life or according to some cynical observers are offering 'other services' under the euphemistic label of 'modelling'.

What I can say from experience is that without exception the young women I have met and photographed have fallen into one of two clear types. Some have been genuine and serious in their aspirations to develop careers in the modelling world with a clear focus and ideas about their way ahead. The majority though have been those in it simply for the fun experience or a way to help build their personal confidence and maybe earn a little pocket money. Indeed, several that I have kept in touch with have gone on to develop serious careers in law or medicine and even now still enjoy a little escapism by dressing up in something frivolous or outlandish to pose for my camera and I thank them for their continued trust and confidence in me. Another one has stepped behind the camera and is now a successful photographer herself.

iv

For Marilyn's birthday this year, we went with our friends Jill and Clive to Italy. The Cinque Terre, meaning "Five Lands" is a coastal area within Liguria, in the northwest of Italy. It lies in the west of La Spezia Province, and comprises the five villages of Monterosso Al Mare, Vernazza, Corniglia, Manarola and Riomaggiore.

On arrival in Pisa, we had picked up a hire car and driven to our accommodation or as near as we could get with a car which was actually some way from the small hotel. We had to park at the top of a hill and carry our bags down the steep slope that was inaccessible by car. Over the centuries, people have built terraces on the rugged, steep landscape right up the cliffs that overlook the Ligurian Sea. Paths, trains and boats connect the villages as cars can reach them from the outside only via narrow and precarious mountain roads with great difficulty. The buildings appear to be stacked one over the other from the waterline up the steep slopes and were a great photographic opportunity for me.

Riomaggiore from the sea

The coastline, the five villages, and the surrounding hillsides are all part of the Cinque Terre National Park, a UNESCO World Heritage Site and a popular tourist destination.

We enjoyed four days wandering the precipitous paths between the lovely old buildings and utilised both the boat and little train to visit the other villages all of which had subtly different characters.

Marilyn's birthday in Italy

On the way back to the airport we called into Carrara where the famous white or grey/white marble is quarried and in Lucca for lunch and to look at the magnificent Basilica of San Michele faced with marble and decorated with the most amazing religious sculptures.

New Year saw us in Heidelberg with some friends for an enjoyable few days of sight-seeing and most importantly the crazy firework festivities. From our friends' description of the "fireworks by the bridge" I had rather imagined that, in true organised English fashion, there would be an official display mounted on the bridge, which would indeed have been a perfect location and provided an impressive spectacle. However, what happened was very different and by our health and safety criteria, downright dangerous.

Basically, anyone could just turn up with as many fireworks as they wished ranging from the relatively innocuous to the heavy-duty pyrotechnics normally used by professionals. As the city is divided by the Necker River the festivities were likewise divided and developed into something akin to a firework battle. People launched rockets from wherever they stood; often simply by holding them in the hand, and while they were not aiming to bombard the opposite bank, in a great many cases that is exactly what happened. As a result, on our side, whilst we enjoyed a very good show, we were also rained on by spent rocket cases. Meanwhile, other attendees on our side simply let off their non-ballistic arsenals in the streets all around us.

The atmosphere was extremely festive and huge fun but again, English to the core, we made a tactical withdrawal to what we regarded as at least a slightly safer distance. In the event, it all went off well if slightly crazily and no-one got hurt which I have to admit surprised me a bit.

While writing this I did wonder if my impressions had perhaps been warped a bit by time so I Googled "German fireworks at New Year" and discovered that this type of behaviour is normal. Below is an extract from a blog called **40percentgerman.com** that rather confirms my conclusions.

"Non-Germans are told that Germany is a land of rules, regulations and order, but as it turns out, New Year's Eve is the exception to the rule. It is a liminal space, where rules exist but are ignored for the sake of a good time, if a good time can be had once you've had a firework explode in your hand. Things may change, but I imagine it will take a long time before anyone prevents the levels of chaos seen on the streets of Germany during New Year.

I am aware that for some, this kind of pearl-clutching is odious and typical of people who want to spoil a good time. I'm not German and I would not have decided to live in Germany if all I wanted to do was complain or change everything to how I think it should be done. That would certainly be a ridiculous and frankly infuriating way to live my life. That's why I usually avoid New Year's celebrations here, if people feel so strongly about their freedom to maim themselves and others, so be it. I may well be clutching my pearls, but at least I can do it with all the fingers I was born with."

v

2014 was a quieter year in terms of travel although all the other activities around The Garden Room B&B, my copy-writing, driving and a bit of continuing handyman stuff still went on. Plus, I was still writing the first memoir and it became the turn of photography for a spell on the back burner.

There was a new interest in our life around this time although to be more precise it was Marilyn's interest and mine only in passing. She had long had a hankering to find out a bit more about bell-ringing – as in church tower bells, so she went along to the church in Shere and introduced herself. They welcomed her with open arms as the band was comprised mostly of older people so new blood like hers was very much sought-after. And that took care of every Thursday evening and an hour or so on Sunday mornings. Meanwhile, in May I had arranged another photographic trip.

This time it was with tutor Jacqui Hurst to the south-west of France not far from Toulouse. I'd done a photo course with Jacqui at West Dean college and this trip was just a kind of continuation of the same.

Run by an English couple Giles and Louise Nevill, the gite complex we stayed in was just outside a village called Daumazan-sur-Arize in the Ariege region and within sight of the Pyrenees. The accommodation was excellent as was the food and Giles had sought out several locations for us to visit and photograph. These included a working watermill where, in the dim interior, we were able to capture atmospheric images of whirring machinery through a haze of flour dust (not brilliant for the cameras).

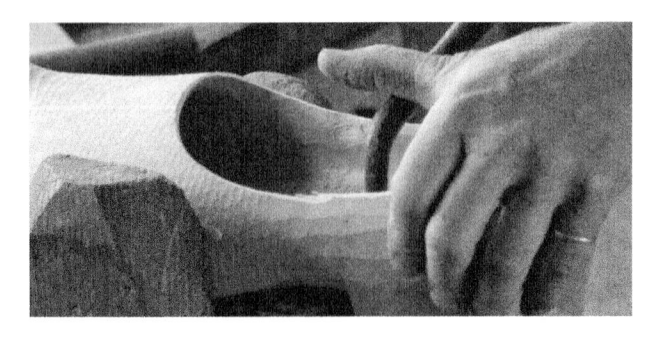

Clog-maker at work

Other outings were to a traditional *sabotier* or wooden clog maker, a wood-fired bakery, a violin maker's workshop and the weekly market at

Mirepoix that offered a fabulous range of candid imagery for the taking. Then one afternoon we were all loaded into the mini-bus and conveyed to a stunning mountain lake surrounded by forest that we were sent off to photograph while Giles attended the barbecue, and the beers cooled in the chill lake water. What an afternoon – idyllic was the only word.

Returning to the gites, we had a large studio available for our use where Jacqui briefed us in advance of the outings and helped with photo processing on our return. Pre-dinner drinks and nibbles were served in the garden prior to superb evening meals by Giles and Louise. I'd go back in a heartbeat provided the photographic itinerary was a bit different. To check it out visit www.manzac.com .

I notice that other special interest holidays are now on offer including, painting, drone photography, nature-study and cycling. (I have since sadly learnt that due to the Covid pandemic, Giles and Louise are selling up and the business is for sale.)

To satisfy those of us interested in portraiture Giles had managed to find Sandrine , a local girl to come in and sit for us. This is between poses. I love catching these unguarded natural moments.

After a quiet summer at home, in September we slipped away again for ten days in France where we flew to Biarritz, rented a car and drove part of the Camino that Marilyn had walked from Le Puy to Conques the previous year. It was so nice to visit with her and hear her recalling the various experiences she'd had along the way.

As if that wasn't enough for her, Marilyn had arranged to go directly from our week together to complete the next section of her second walk to Santiago. So, after a night in the hotel back at Biarritz, at the crack of dawn, I set off for my flight back to home and domestic duties while she caught a train to Aire Sur l'Adur to walk the final section of the French route that would take her over the Pyrenees and into Spain. I cannot overstate how proud I am of my wife and her sheer determination when it came to the Camino.

21   2015 A QUIETER YEAR

i

This year was going to be quieter, at least as far as travel was concerned. The reason for this is that my wife is a great planner and organiser.

We had for some time talked about including Cuba in our agenda of travel plans but frankly (and to my shame I must confess); if these things were left to me, we probably wouldn't do that much at all. I have to admit to having a more laid back, not to say lackadaisical attitude to certain things, and if not 'encouraged by management' probably would never get around to organising anything. So the plan was laid almost a year ahead that in January 2016 we would go, and because it was going to be expensive, we had decided that our activity during 2015 would have to be a bit more limited.

Frankly, this didn't bother me too much as I can usually fill my time with something or other. Whether it was finalising the second edition of the book, ploughing through a few genealogical records or getting out with the camera and dog, I felt quite relaxed about it.

However, we did both have plans for one trip each to further our individual interests. Marilyn had another Camino lined up for September and I had a photographic week or so in Wales beginning to take shape.

I set off in May to South Wales, the intention being, in addition to my usual landscape photography, to have a look at some of the former industrial sites like the coal mines and steelworks in The Valleys. To that end, I had booked a hotel in Ebbw Vale for three nights which I thought should be long enough.

With a history dating back to 1790, iron and coal were inextricably linked in Ebbw Vale with the formation of the Ebbw Vale Steel, Iron and Coal Company. The availability of limestone along with coal and iron ore in the vicinity made the valley a prime candidate for the developing industry. Both industries experienced highs and lows over the years culminating in its final reinvention as the largest tinplate producer in the country before its closure in 2002.

I hoped to capture some gritty and poignant images of the industrial landscape but I was too late as the flat-bottomed valley that was once occupied by the mile-long steelworks was empty. The only remains I saw of the vanished industry were a monstrous steel rolling mill left as a monument to what had once been and an attractive Victorian building that had been the pay and admin office for the site.

The scale of this monster mill can be judged by comparison with the trees and my car beside it.

There was some new build including Blaenau Gwent's cutting-edge Learning Zone intended to become the home of all A-Level education in the county. The Learning Zone is part of the regeneration of the former steelworks site in Ebbw Vale that also includes the highly modern-looking Sports Centre.

Another innovation intended to compensate for the pain and unemployment caused by the closure of the works was the inauguration of Festival Park. This comprised a beautifully landscaped leisure park and fishing lakes together with a mall of outlet shopping with ample free parking. It was quiet, untidy and going to seed when I visited and I understood from people I spoke with that the main impact had been the destruction of what had remained of the town centre economy due mainly to the regional and central governments failing to consult adequately to determine the real local needs.

A final scheme that is still just about rumbling on but with little prospect of success (for lack of investment capital) is the creation of a new international motor racing circuit along with all the infrastructure and commercial development required to support the idea. All in all, I felt Ebbw Vale was still mourning its lost past and with very little sign of strong recovery. Just seven miles away around the hill from Ebbw Vale is Blaenavon where I intended to visit the Big Pit National Coal Museum. This was a worthwhile excursion.

Apart from being able to see the preserved above-ground infrastructure including the big winding gear, workshops, miners' canteens and so on, the visit included a descent into the mine in the cage-lift with the miner's helmet and lamp.

Not good for claustrophobics but fascinating to get a real insight into the coal mining experience especially as our guide was a former miner.

Other places of interest in the area included the steam train ride from Big Pit to Blaenavon town, beautiful Bedwellty House and Park in Tredegar and the lovely walk along the valley to the impressive Neath waterfalls.

To be fair, I would not describe the area as uplifting but it's certainly worth a visit for anyone at all interested in our industrial heritage.

My second planned B&B location was down on the Gower peninsular, an area known for its beautiful landscapes and it had been on my visit list for some time. However, it didn't get off the greatest start because on arrival I was greeted with the news that there was neither heating nor hot water. It seemed the fuel oil tank had sprung a leak overnight and several hundred gallons of oil was in the process of leaking into a local watercourse.

Both fire brigade and heating installation engineers were all over the shop with pumps and so on trying to avoid pollution by recovering as much as they could before the low-loader was due to arrive with a new tank. I was advised everything should be fine but would I mind going off for two or three hours. I took myself for coffee and a sandwich at the excellent community shop in Llanmadoc village. Manned by volunteers it provided the full range of services from mini-market and post-office to café and community hub.

Suitably refreshed, I set off to explore and found my way to Port Eynon beach. Situated on the most southerly point of the Gower, it is thought to be named after an Eleventh Century Welsh Prince, Eynon. Once there was a booming trade in oyster production, limestone quarrying, lobstering and crabbing, not to mention a significant amount of smuggling. At one stage, it is thought that eight excise men were stationed in the village alone.

At the far end of Port Eynon beach stands the Eighteenth-Century ruin of the old salt house. Originally extracting salt from the sea, it is thought that the business was run as a cover for smuggled goods. Maybe this theory is not too far-fetched when you consider that most of the local population of the 16th, 17th and 18th centuries appeared to have been involved in smuggling. On one notable occasion, the contraband goods were hidden in the church.

In the churchyard is a memorial to the three lifeboat crew members who lost their lives at sea in 1916. The lifeboat station was closed in 1919 when it was considered too dangerous to be located in Port Eynon.

A new lifeboat station was opened in Horton in 1968. Below the cliff where the castle is once believed to have stood, is Culver Hole. This rather unusual cave, between two rock faces, has a masonry wall. There is a staircase inside that leads up to four floors. Legend links it to the castle and also as a safe hideaway for contraband, but today it is inhabited by pigeons and seagulls. (Credit for the above text to Gower Holidays website)

Back at the B&B, amazingly the new tank had arrived, been installed, connected and filled and hot water was on tap. I wished that back home we could have achieved such service. After a very comfortable night and a hearty breakfast, I set out for more exploring.

Just meandering around the lanes was a delight with stunning vistas opening up at almost every turn especially close to the coast. Chief of these was the dramatic view along the 3-mile beach at Rhossilli. There is not a lot to the village but the very large National Trust car park is evidence enough that the place gets busy in season. Fortunately, it was relatively quiet when I was there and I enjoyed the level one kilometre walk along the cliff path to the old coastguard station for even better views of Wormshead point and the lines of surf rolling into Rhossilli Bay. My camera was well employed.

Beautiful Rhossili Beach on the Gower Peninsular

To the north of Llanmadoc, the 4-mile-wide estuary of the River Loughor extends inland for some 6 miles and includes hundreds of hectares of salt marsh and wetland. It is possible to walk out for some distance towards the main central channel and well-trodden paths are adequately bridged where they cross smaller side channels and rifes. Care would be needed I suspect in times of extra high tides as, like many such wetlands, the water level can rise surprisingly fast. When I visited the weather was ideal and there was a lot of livestock grazing freely including some large groups of horses which in that scenery reminded me strongly of the Camargue in the south of France.

In June we went briefly out to our Spanish flat with some friends and enjoyed showing them around some of our favourite places, and then in August, I took the camera along to a couple of local events. These were the Medieval Fair and Joust at Loxwood and the classic car show at Cranleigh, both of which allowed me to get a good selection of further images.

22   A LONG-HAUL TRIP
AND MORE PHOTOGRAPHY

i

When I was still working and for a few years after I left the police, we were a bit better off than later on and did quite a bit of travel to some of the far-flung places described.   However more recently our travel has been frequent but a bit more local as in Europe and North Africa.

To be honest, while there are many places I would have liked to visit, I haven't missed the long flights which I find boring and uncomfortable. I am fascinated by the technology of flight so I love boarding a plane, the take-offs and landings and can watch in fascination as the wing flaps operate during the climb to cruising height (yes, I'm a bit odd) but after that, I'm done, especially if its more than a couple of hours.

So, our long-planned trip to Cuba in January 2016 was the first in a long time and we were both very excited despite the prospect of a ten-hour flight. We'd signed up with Rickshaw Travel, a small independent company in Brighton who were excellent and whose staff had all been to the various places they sold so it was possible to have first-hand information about the travel experience a particular destination could offer.

With their help, we were able to more or less tailor-make our itinerary covering the interests we had and the time available as well as our budget. One of their advisors suggested that as we can both speak a bit of Spanish we might get more out of the whole experience if we stayed with local families rather than the few but expensive state hotels. She told us that at least we would have good home-cooked food genuinely typical of the country and even if it would not be exactly a gourmet experience it would be wholesome plus we would experience a bit of real Cuban life.

Virgin Atlantic was brilliant, even in economy, at least in comparison to the budget flights we had been used to. The cabin crew were polite, smart and efficient; we had more than enough films on offer to fill the time we weren't sleeping and we even had a real meal included. Couldn't really ask for more.

Frozen wastes from thirty-nine thousand feet.

Of course, with long haul when traversing long distance around the globe we do not travel in straight lines although actually we do. Confused? Logically I would have thought that to arrive in the Caribbean from London one would go west or even south-west, however, we didn't. Our flight headed out north-west in what is known as a 'great circle route' so that we found ourselves flying over the frozen wastes of Newfoundland and eventually running parallel down the east coast of Florida to arrive in Havana.

It feels counter-intuitive but it is a navigational peculiarity. Planes fly in straight lines through three-dimensional space and although travelling by the shortest route it appears curved when drawn across the globe. Just thought I'd throw that in as it intrigued me. Told you several times that I'm a bit odd.

It was almost midnight local time when we emerged from José Marti International Airport in Havana where we had arranged for a taxi to the hotel. Wanting to get into the Cuban mood as soon as possible I had asked for one of the famous American 1950's classic cars so we drove in grand style in this white and rather tired Cadillac convertible the nine miles or so into the city.

Our hotel was charming in a run-down kind of way. Very much Spanish colonial in style with large elegant rooms, high ceilings, balconies and slatted shutters; it was pretty much identical to all the other buildings on the street albeit perhaps in slightly better repair. We hit the sack.

A good thing about digital photography is that every image is time and date stamped so I can tell you that by 8.40 the same morning we had eaten our rolls and coffee and were wandering around a nearby square admiring the faded grandeur of the architecture while a couple of primary school classes were having their PE lessons. It was a complete flash-back for me to my own time in school in the fifties where there was a bit of kindly and purposeful discipline and everyone was better for it – and fitter too. Someone explained it was one of the hangovers of the communist regime where state control reached into every aspect of life.

The streets of Havana were vibrant, dirty and fascinating in equal measure. Along with the buildings, clothes were bright if a bit tired; traffic was not so very busy and included a complete range of vehicles from the aged gas-guzzling American cars of the fifties to the slightly more recent communist Trabant. There were bubble cars, exhaust belching motorcycle sidecar combinations, cycle rickshaws, horses and horse-drawn taxis. It was fabulous for its variety.

While we had heard about the now legendary American classic cars to be found in Cuba, nothing had prepared us for the numbers. They may be rare in the US but not in Cuba where there are thousands and it is an incredible tribute to the numerous backstreet repair workshops that have had to find ways to keep the things on the road for 60 years in the face of the US embargo preventing the import of spares (even if they could be found).

A typical Havana street scene.

I cannot possibly relate our total experience around the streets of Havana; perhaps best if you have a moment, to check out 'Havana or Cuba – Google images'. Sufficient to say we did as much as we could to soak up the history of the Castro – Guevara revolution, visited the important sites and museums, gained an understanding of America's despicable role in Cuban history, took the bus trips but most rewardingly, we simply wandered.

One significant development that is worth a mention is that whatever America may want, Havana is well and truly on the Caribbean cruise itinerary as a port of call and when we were there was hosting three or four enormous cruise ships no doubt bringing welcome cash to the locals.

An amazing portrait of
Fidel Castro we found in a
museum

After a couple of days in the capital, we visited the Viñales region where most of the country's tobacco is grown. Here we stayed as suggested in a family house, not much different in principle to the bed and breakfast operation of our own in Surrey. The house was owned by a couple who were absolutely charming and welcoming and it was here that we gained a bit more understanding about Cuba.

With its communist background, Cuba has had excellent health and education systems although we understood they are groaning a bit now. Where the thing falls down is that due to the economic isolation brought about by sanctions there is very little work at a professional level. Agriculture yes, tobacco tending and cigar rolling yes, but teacher, scientist, doctor, not likely and certainly no future in politics all the while the Castro family are around.

As an example of this, our lovely hostess Niulvys was a qualified engineering professor but could find no work in either education or industry which was why they were running their private home as a guest house. I thought that was so sad.

We had arranged in advance to do a horse ride around the tobacco plantations but the weather had been so wet that many of the tracks were impassable so our hosts had organised an alternative trip around the area including a tobacco farm and cigar factory. Our alternative transport was a huge red nineteen-fifties Chevrolet. There was no ignition switch so the car had to be hot-wired each time to start the engine and behind the substantial leather front bench seat, I noticed a steel tube had been welded from one side to the other and appeared to be there to hold the car together. Anyway, we did the tour and survived but I guess you are beginning to get a little feel for the country now.

After a couple of days in Viñales, we moved on to an area known as Las Terrazas which is the centre for a huge environmental regeneration project. It is located in the Sierra del Rosario mountains and designated a UNESCO Biosphere Reserve.

The village has a population of about 1,000 with several hotels and restaurants catering for tourists. The nature reserve includes 5000 hectares of secondary forest which was planted on the surrounding (deforested) hills by building terraces to avoid erosion; hence the name. The reserve is rich in flora and fauna and includes lakes, rivers, and waterfalls. Organised excursions on the many footpaths and trails can be booked at the local tourist office. In addition to the forestry work, the locals are mostly self-employed in eco-tourism, art or craft activities such as papermaking and printing.

Trinidad and Cienfuegos were both fascinating towns in their way and we enjoyed a couple of days in each and being whisked between our various reserved lodgings by the prompt and efficient private taxi service arranged from the UK.

As this was our first time in the Caribbean, we thought that perhaps we should have a few beach days although that is not really our style. So we had arranged to have three days in Varadero the main beach resort of the island. It didn't go well because although the sea was the right sort of azure blue and the beaches white, the surf was huge and too dangerous to venture into at all and it remained the same for the whole three days we were there. I guess you can't win them all. Just as well we're not beach addicts.

ii

The following month I went to Vaughantown. Now, this was an interesting experience and was the second time I had been. It's only mentioned in this chapter because of the Spanish language connection.

Vaughantown is a gathering organised by Vaughan Systems, an English language teaching company started by American Richard Vaughan in the seventies. The largest English Language teaching firm in Spain, Vaughan invites volunteers to spend six days in Spain in a unique cultural exchange program between English speakers of any nationality and Spanish professionals in a fun language-learning and self-growth experience.

This volunteer program in Spain is open to all native English speakers who are naturally inquisitive, enjoy nature and the outdoors, and are outgoing, open and friendly. It's typically composed of 15 Spaniards and 15 English speakers who together spend a week sharing long conversations, participating in skits, theatre, games and outdoor activities.

For the volunteers, the up-side is the opportunity to stay free of charge in a four-star hotel in Spain with all meals and drinks included while they meet, chat and socialise in English with Spanish business people who want to learn English. There is no actual teaching involved but you may do a degree of correction if you wish. It is quite handy if you know a bit of English grammar because the students seemed quite keen on understanding the grammar and could ask some testing questions. You could of course always refer them to the tutor but it would seem a bit of a cop-out. The down-side is that it is quite tiring especially if you try to keep up with the Spaniards in the bar after hours. The only cost to the volunteers is the price of a flight to Madrid and the first night in a hotel before meeting the course directors the following morning. However, even the cost of this night is discounted if the hotel suggested by Vaughan is used.

The actual venues are not located in Madrid but in other towns of the region and are usually places of historic interest or landscape beauty. On this occasion, the venue was a fabulously restored medieval palace with vast luxurious rooms, a swimming pool and gardens and a magnificent colonnaded courtyard that had been roofed over and was used as the main dining room It was about a two-hour drive from Madrid in the small town of Belmonte in Cuenca province. Some volunteers have become regulars and sometimes combine a week with Vaughan with another week or two exploring Madrid itself or elsewhere. A shrewd way to get a free holiday within a holiday.

I used to walk a short distance to these mills to catch the incredible sunsets.

Returning from Cuba, I had a sizeable batch of photographs to edit which fortunately I enjoy. As well as the more or less obligatory landscape images from such a trip I had also done pretty well with street and people photography. This was an interest that had started sometime before but the Cuba trip had provided ample opportunity for practising this genre.

I got a lot more practice photographing people one weekend in June when the parish council asked me to do the photography for the village event to mark The Queen's 90th birthday. It was a lovely weekend and the sun shone as the villagers celebrated with a street party. Long tables were laid up in front of the village hall and plates of party food were handed out to one and all. A Union Jack cake made by a local resident was ceremoniously cut by the vicar. The pub and village store did a roaring trade and honestly, it would have been hard to visualise a more archetypal if somewhat idealised image of English village living. And I was there with my trusty Nikon camera to record it all for posterity or the parish mag at least.

I'd heard about a course being run at West Dean in June that sounded appropriate for me at that time. It was called "People and Places" and was looking in-depth at photographing people in context. The tutor was Jacqui Hurst who I did the course with in France a couple of years before. Among many other types of photography, she does a lot of work for crafts-people; capturing images of them at work in their various studios and workshops practising their crafts. The photographs were mainly used for their web pages. She certainly knew her stuff though about introducing people into images.

I was fascinated and once I started including people in my general images, be they landscape or candid street shots I just couldn't get enough of it. A street is always interesting and a beautiful landscape will be beautiful today and tomorrow and forever; and provided the technique is correct, will yield impressive images. However, once there is a person in the frame the dynamic changes and it starts to create a story, either obvious or often more subtle. What is that person's tale? Who and what are they? Where are they going, doing, thinking and so on? I was captivated and have been a keen collector of candid street images ever since.

A trick that Jacqui taught us was to stand still instead of wandering about. She said *"If I could I'd nail your foot to the ground."* because the natural thing to do is to move around 'looking' for the subject, but in her view, the better technique is to identify a suitable background and lighting situation and then wait for your subject to walk "into the frame" so to speak. It also benefits from the fact that you can have the camera set up for light and so only have to concentrate on focus and framing once the person arrives. I tried and it works but it's not very natural if you are the type of person who wants to be moving along all the time.

A fortunate candid capture on Littlehampton promenade.

iii

In August, I'm almost embarrassed to say that we were off again and this despite our best intentions to have a frugal travel year. It really is very addictive. This time it was to Ghent for a short break with close friends Jill and Clive.

What a lovely city and a photographer's dream. Of course, why else would I be there? It was only a long weekend trip so naturally we were limited with what we could do but as ever we managed to squeeze in quite a bit.

Located about twenty (crow's flight) miles inland from the North Sea; Ghent is a port city in northwest Belgium, at the confluence of the Leie and Scheldt rivers. During the Middle Ages, it was a prominent city-state. Today it's a university town and cultural hub. Its pedestrianised centre is known for medieval architecture such as the 12th-century Gravensteen castle and the Graslei, a row of guildhalls beside the Leie river harbour.

Architecturally Ghent is a delight especially when taken together with the various canals and waterways that add so much to the visual impact, particularly at night.

The city is also well known for its large public squares and marketplaces, chief among which is the Vrijdagmarkt (Friday Market), the centre of the life of the medieval city.

The food was good and interesting too and we sampled the range from fast food on the street to a Michelin level restaurant that Jill had researched in advance. The river trip was well worth doing and provided a very different photographic perspective of the waterside buildings as well as the opportunity for some interesting candid shots of people.

Far from a crafty candid shot as this hen party were almost begging to be photographed having fun.

I know I said 2016 was supposed to be a year of much less travel but shortly after Ghent we decided to take a quick trip to the flat courtesy of EasyJet's ridiculously low prices to attend a medieval fair in a neighbouring town. It's an event we had been to before and always enjoyed, plus it was good to catch up with our Spanish friends Cris and Fernando and of course a great photo opportunity.

Sadly, while there we heard that a very dear and elderly friend had died. Gwen was a very special lady who had for years been the telephonist at police HQ in Guildford and Marilyn had met when she first went there to work in the control room. Marilyn and Gwen had become very close, pretty much the daughter Gwen had never had and over many years they even holidayed together. I met her when I first went to work at HQ in the Press Office and it was her that introduced me to Marilyn so she was delighted when our friendship flourished.

Gwen had been in the vanguard of British tourism to Spain and used to drive down with her husband and another couple to the Costa Brava when the area was just beginning to open up to foreign visitors in the late sixties. So, there was an added common interest when Marilyn and I developed an affinity for Catalunya ourselves.

She was a London girl whose father was a police sergeant and apparently a bit of a hard task-master so when Gwen was evacuated to Surrey during the war, she was in no hurry to go back and made the Guildford area her home. She was a clippie on the local buses for many years and also a GPO telephonist which I guess is how she gained the experience to apply for the job at Surrey HQ.

Gwen the 'clippie'; Gwen the voice of Surrey Constabulary; Gwen's retirement from HQ; and with Marilyn after she went into a retirement home coincidentally just a few yards from the police HQ.

Gwen Kidder – a very dear friend and colleague

Gwen's passing was very much the end of an era, both for us as a couple and for many of the Surrey Constabulary staff to whom she had become Auntie Gwen.

November saw me once again heading for Spain but this time on my own and back to Galicia. The main objective was to catch up with friends Anna and Lluis and to meet for the first time their little daughter Thomasina. I was also planning to do some photography around the Sil Canyon where they live but also in Santiago city.

Little Thomy was an absolute delight and it was so nice to see that despite Lluis being a good bit older than most parents of a four-year-old he was no less besotted than any other father.

I have some lovely photos of Thomy with Anna and Lluis and I must confess to feeling very emotional around the fact that without our involvement in Lluis's life all those years before, that beautiful child would never have been born. It does make one think a bit about those many tiny decision points in life that we generally take so lightly.

Santiago was great too and the weather fine for a change, so I came away with even more images for the archive.

23 MORE WRITING AND A POSSIBLE MOVE

i

After Stepping Out from Ashtead was first published in 2015, I was quite gratified by the positive response; and if not exactly deafened by critical acclaim, I was quietly pleased with myself, not to mention the few pounds of royalties it paid most months. It was this slight success and the fact that I very much enjoyed the creative process that decided me to go ahead and write the sequel that would cover the next thirty years of my life.

I probably started this around the end of 2015 and although both the writing and photography took alternate turns on the back burner, I was able to make good progress and had the first draft complete by around the middle of 2017. At the same time, I had been making some minor revisions to the first book in the light of comments various readers had made and additions that had come to mind in the interim.

The second book, apart from including the four years after I left the Met when I sold cars, was going to be about my career as a police officer in Surrey. I had to think quite hard about the sort of line to follow because I wanted it to be different. There are any number of police memoirs by celebrated and some *'not so celebrated but think they are'* retired officers that are self-serving lists of cases that tell a story of individuals who believe they were great 'thief-takers', 'crime-busters' or big movers in other ways.

Well, I was certainly not that sort of police officer in fact in many ways I was a bit of a square peg in the service. While many of my colleagues were quite physical and liked nothing better than mixing it with the local yobs, I tended to avoid such confrontation preferring the less aggressive approach.

(Writing this, instead of 'yobs' I was going to use the expression 'tow-rag', a common term in the job for bad boys, criminals and the like. However, on checking its derivation I decided against it but now understand why in some cases its use does seem rather appropriate. I'll leave you to look it up for yourself. Sufficient to say it has a lavatorial naval origin.)

Nor was I what in common parlance these days is called a 'team player', which the police service certainly needs. Quite the opposite in fact, as my preferred work style was either individual or a very small team. However, in any organization, there is a place for most types to make their mark as I believe I did in a variety of interesting and challenging specialist roles if not so much in operational policing.

I wanted to tell the story of an ordinary guy but a very ambitious one. A man who worked hard and gave of his best in the professional arena whilst also being a family man working hard on the home front to keep a shaky marriage together but ultimately failing. So, it was to be a highly personal story and as I believe a memoir should above all else be honest, it would also of necessity at times have to be against myself.

Here is not the place to reiterate the story when it's already been told in the book, but I will explain why it was entitled Until the Lights Went Out.

While my police service was for the most part enjoyable and successful it was at times frustrating which is a normal element of most people's working life. However, out of work my domestic situation was a huge challenge over several years eventually resulting in a somewhat acrimonious divorce and custody proceedings that left me in charge of two young children. Whilst this was the outcome I had wanted; it did somewhat limit my career opportunities as I couldn't be available for the full range of shift duties, a fact that added to my general stress levels.

Following a few years on my own, I remarried and happily have remained so. During the early years of our relationship, following an inheritance Marilyn and I embarked on an ambitious house-building project. Unfortunately, due to my over-ambitious ideas it went so over-budget that we couldn't afford to live in the dream home we had built. Rightly or wrongly, I viewed this as a total failure of judgment, mostly on my part, not to mention a huge anticlimax and disappointment. The last straw was on the work front when the senior colleague I was sharing a responsible role with was removed without replacement.

Management was deaf to his and my warnings that it would not work and I lasted just over a month.

In February '94 I suffered a catastrophic emotional break-down that pitched me into a deep depression and a six-month period of which I have virtually no recollection, an almost total blank in my life. Hence the title - Until the Lights Went Out.

If all this sounds impossibly depressing, I should say that it does not represent the whole book which contains any number of much lighter, amusing and often hilarious stories from my brief time as a 1960's motor trade and then a police officer. It also makes interesting reading as it lifts the veil on a number of my specialist roles that are little known by the public and that the average bobby doesn't get to experience.

So that in brief is how the second memoir got underway and then early in 2018 was published and hit the Amazon lists.

I had a lot of very positive feedback on the book from serving and former police officers in Surrey and elsewhere. The main responses expressed admiration for my honesty and courage in publishing what, as I said before, were my own shortcomings as well as achievements. Several former colleagues also said how they could identify with many of the situations I described, both on the work and domestic fronts. To me, the feedback revealed the high levels of concealed stress some of my colleagues were, and presumably, still are having to manage just to keep afloat.

ii

It was probably also around 2015 that my health started to give cause for concern. Apart from what might be described as usual issues affecting men of a certain age such as hernia and prostate operations plus the odd A and E visits, I have enjoyed good health all my life. So, when my heart started to misbehave, I have to admit it came as a bit of a shock.

The reason for the surprise was two-fold. Firstly, because I have made an effort to pursue a relatively active and mobile lifestyle, indeed for most of the eight years or so that I worked at police HQ I was running about four miles a day.

The second factor is that the heart has a significance way above other organs, so to be told I had a problem really hit home. In my mind, this was because I have two of most other important organs but only one heart. Apparently, the medical profession acknowledges this situation and doctors are trained to be especially careful when announcing such diagnoses.

My actual issue is atrial fibrillation which in many people affects them very little if it is even noticed at all. However, for me, the irregularity and very fast but inefficient heart rate robs me of energy and leaves me unable to operate at what I regard as an acceptable level.

Ironically it turns out that all that 'healthy' running I did may have contributed to the problem by overdeveloping the output side of my heart muscle which is another part of the problem I now have. I have also learnt that the knee issues I've had were probably also contributed to by the running. Funny old world isn't it?

I have had several procedures which do correct the problem for a while but as the cardio man said these are likely to offer progressively shorter periods of relief and in the longer term, he would probably be looking at a pacemaker.

So, like many others of my vintage, I shall just keep taking the tablets and be grateful that we do at least have a system that doesn't require me to re-mortgage my home to pay for them.

iii

We loved our years in Peaslake with the B&B, my various self-employed activities, Marilyn's job at the Hurtwood Inn hotel and her bell-ringing, all the relationships we made and the life we had there. So why on earth would we think of moving?

There were several reasons. One was no more or less than 'itchy feet' and a desire for a change of scenery. Another was the fact that while the house ticked the boxes in many ways there were aspects that we still weren't totally happy with but which we couldn't change, at least not with the funds we had. We were also conscious that the house, having been built in the 1930s, was at some point going to need a new roof which would have been a huge cost and that whatever we did to it the thermal efficiency could never really be much improved beyond what we had already done.

Although only semi-retired at that time (early 2015), we were mindful that the years were moving on and that a reduction in work would also bring a reduced income so another revenue stream would be useful. This was where our purchase of the Peaslake house and Marilyn's assessment of its potential offered us an opportunity.

There is a huge premium attaching to property in the Surrey Hills that made our modest three-bed bungalow worth a good bit more than it would have been as little as just six miles down the road. It was this that we decided to capitalize on. We thought that by moving we could almost certainly find a property offering the same or even better accommodation but also release enough money to buy a flat to rent out for income. But where would this new home be?

You'll remember that when I left the police we moved to Sussex; so that was one area we knew quite well, not just from that time but from all those childhood years of trips around and through Sussex to the seaside. There was a huge and comfortable familiarity there.

But perhaps we could be a bit bolder; move even further out and achieve an even larger cash return by going where property was very cheap. So, we started to think about the possibilities. This was going to be tricky because we are incredibly blessed in the south-east in terms of convenience. Firstly, we have the capital close at hand with all its historical and cultural relevance and although we don't visit often, it is very good to know we can.

However, for us the main benefit that would be extremely hard to do without would be the communications. As you've read, we are a couple that loves to travel and so the excellent (although often frustrating) road network, proximity to the channel ports and most importantly the three or four airports are all very important to us.

We did head out on several exploratory sorties to places like Norfolk and Suffolk, the west country (but definitely not as far as Cornwall) and even out to Hereford and the borders but always they just felt too far and poorly connected. I guess it was also the effect of our Surrey roots.

It's funny; we may think we are 'citizens of the world' who could make a home anywhere but as we found on our ultimately unsuccessful attempt to move to Spain it's not that easy. In the event, we felt the most comfortable option and that which would also free up enough cash could be achieved in Sussex once again. We'd lived there before and knew we liked it. And it was also far enough out to feel just that bit less frenetic than Surrey, much of which has nowadays become almost a London suburb.

24   A SOFT LANDING

i

I hate moving house now. Our previous experiences, of which there have been several, have all gone relatively easily; as in quite quickly and more or less without a hitch, so I guess we were a bit naïve in anticipating that history would naturally repeat itself.

While our location in the Surrey Hills was indeed very desirable it turned out that our house was less so. The feedback was that the rooms were too small for most people as the trend has apparently moved away from 'cosy' towards a more open-plan layout, and to be fair, a larger living room was also on our wish list of features for a new home.

We had many enquiries and viewings and while it seemed the garden was a big plus point, it was still the interior space that put people off. Naturally, when the property first went on the market we were also looking around for our own next home and went to see several 'possibles', most of which didn't come up to the brochure descriptions once seen in the flesh so to speak.

The agent continued to be confident that our buyer would soon appear but after several months with no sale in view we were so demoralised that we stopped viewing properties ourselves, deciding that until we had an offer it was a pointless exercise. We had the house sold a couple of times only to have buyers pull out for various reasons although we had one who seemed very keen but then made such a derisory offer that we couldn't even consider it. Unfortunately, by that time we had our eyes on a house in the small town of Storrington.

The house was lovely and had recently been extended and refurbished to a virtually 'brand new' specification. We were bowled over and told the vendor we were seriously interested but he would not consider an offer until ours was also under offer. In the event, the house was sold to someone else which in retrospect was probably a good thing because it was actually much larger and more expensive than we needed. I think this was probably another one of those 'guardian angel' interventions that kept us out of trouble.

A few weeks later we found another buyer who seemed in a position to complete quite quickly. We hit the listings again and went off to see a couple of properties, one of which caught our eye. It was a three-bedroom bungalow in a small residential cul de sac and just about an eight-minute walk from the village centre in Storrington where there were more than enough amenities for our purpose.

One of our key requirements was to have basic shops within walking distance as we'd had quite enough of having to jump in the car to get a bottle of milk or other basic need – like a Kit Kat.

The house itself was in superb decorative order having been almost totally refurbished to a very high standard by the vendors whose reason for moving was rather sad. An older couple, they had come together about three years previously and as far as the husband was concerned it was his forever home. Consequently, he had done everything to last. Sadly for him, his partner then changed her mind about the relationship and they decided to separate and so the house went up for sale.

We made an offer which was accepted and we thought, at last, we were home and dry but then once again our own buyer pulled out for lack of finance. To our amazement, the vendors said they would take the house off the market for a month for us to see if another buyer could be found for ours. We were stunned as such humanity and fair-dealing seem to be pretty rare commodities in the world these days and especially within the house buying scene.

We were not hopeful given our experience. The house had been on the market for about eighteen months and the market was depressed due to uncertainty over the BREXIT negotiations so there was nothing we could do to change things other than wait. So we decided to go on holiday and took ourselves off to Greece for a couple of weeks. About halfway through our trip, the agent contacted us to say that the punter who had made the low offer we rejected the previous year had returned with another much more reasonable one. We knew the guy had been very keen to come to Peaslake for family reasons so we suggested the agent reject the offer again to which to guy responded with a full price. Result!! We eventually moved to Storrington in West Sussex in July 2017.

At the time of writing this page we have been living in Storrington for just over four years and have settled into the area very well. The house has turned out to be all we expected. While the garden is much smaller than we were used to it does pretty much all we need. The slight reservation being that Marilyn finds it a little small as she has continued her interest in a bit of vegetable gardening which all has to be done in pots and containers. However, it is pretty well future proof from the point of view that when we feel less able or inclined to grow our own stuff, the garden is otherwise very easy to manage.

The only part of the house the previous owners had not dealt with was the very small 1970's style kitchen. It was well fitted and impeccably clean so in that sense perfectly adequate. However, we had been accustomed to having a fairly generous kitchen/diner and did not enjoy making part of our new and spacious living room into a dining space. So we decided to extend to create the large kitchen/diner we wanted together with a decent utility space and dog room.

Without going into the entire saga, sufficient to say that we chose the wrong builder. We can't deny he was quite a good carpenter and kitchen fitter but not great when it came to a whole extension. Following its supposed completion, the drains blocked due to building debris he had left in them and then the roof leaked.

By this time, he was failing to communicate at all and we had to get another roofing contractor. He took one look and said it was a disastrous job and would need completely re-doing at a cost of £2000. Don't even start me on the role of the building inspector who signed the job off without actually inspecting the roof because he had no ladder! Yes, it takes some believing. They acknowledged their fault and refunded part of the fee.

We ended up taking the builder to court only to find when the bailiffs attended to enforce the judgement that he had left the marital home which was conveniently not in his name but we were also in a queue of potential creditors to who he owed money. So, in the end we had to put it down to experience and move on.

Apart from the unfortunate building experience we love living here. The village has turned out to be as convenient as we expected with more than enough local services to meet our needs. We have the coast a few minutes away plus the airport and channel ports easily on hand. I have an absolute wealth of local landscape to photograph and am building up connections with a few people to help me develop the modelling and portrait work. Marilyn has also made a number of new local connections to meet her various interests.

Most of the Covid restrictions have now been lifted although I do have reservation as the infections and hospitalisations are on the rise again in some areas. (September 2021) However, as we have both had our vaccinations, we have gradually resumed most of our usual activity alongside maintaining a sensible level of caution.

On the travel front, we were until recently restricted under the government's 'traffic light' system which meant that travel and return rules from some countries could change at very short notice. This has also been relaxed so we expect to be using our several times deferred Easyjet tickets in a few weeks time to get out to our place in Spain at long last.

Well dear reader, it appears that we have come to the end of the road and our time together. Thank you so much for staying the course and I hope you have found it an interesting tale. Apart from satisfying myself with the enjoyment I derive from the writing experience I wanted to illustrate that even after a knockback like I experienced when I left the police, it is possible to bounce back and have some fun. I certainly have. If I have a lesson to offer it would be to travel with an open mind and be prepared to have a go at things as they arise. You really never do know where it might lead.

If you want to come back to me with any comment, constructive criticism or questions I welcome reader comment and feedback via e-mail to brianseye@outlook.com I wish you well in your future travels wherever they may lead.

If you thought this was the end of the book, so did I until something happened that rocked my world.

25 SURPRISE, SURPRISE !

i

As a structural tool the classic 'twist in the tale' is a go-to option for authors especially in the realm of fiction, but I guess less so in the memoir genre. That is, unless it is presented without option, which is what happened to me a couple of months back, just as I thought I was putting this book to bed.

In short; totally out of the blue I discovered I had a brother whom I'd never met and who I never will as he passed away in 2015. As you might imagine the shock was profound, followed by a deep sadness that only became greater as I discovered more about the man, weirdly also a Brian, and the circumstances around his birth.

It began with a message from my cousin Gail in Ireland, who you may recall I mentioned previously as having been adopted at birth. She explained that in her continued quest to discover her roots and any extended family she had taken a DNA test offered by one of the organisations providing the online genealogy research system.

Gail told me she had received a message from a Marcus Peck in

Australia who had also done the DNA test and it appeared to show that he and Gail were related because his late father was her cousin. Marcus went on to explain that his father Brian Peck had spent a good part of his life trying to discover his birth history, sadly without success. All he had known was that he was born in St Albans England in May 1941 and given up for adoption. He understood that his mother was an Irish nurse whose surname was Hurson. He further knew that his birth name was John but following his adoption, he became Brian Peck and later moved with his adoptive mother to New Zealand.

After Brian died in 2015 his son Marcus had continued to pursue enquiries without success until he decided to have the DNA test with the results just described.

Gail worked out that if Brian Peck was her cousin, then his mother had to be her aunt which took her back to just three possible females, one of which was my own mother. Of the three, at the time in question, the eldest, my aunt Peggy was a nun, another was already married with two sons, so leaving Ellen Hurson who was at that time unmarried. Logically the only possibility. Well, you can imagine the tricks this played with the imagination of my sister Angela and me.

To have always believed one is a first-born and then have that assumption challenged or destroyed was traumatic to say the least. How could it be? My parents weren't married until a year later, did they even know each other? Who was the father? Was this interloper a brother or a half-brother?

I think initially I was in denial and found myself dreaming up the wildest possible alternative explanations like some imposter or distant lost relative falsely giving my mother's name to divert attention from herself. Why St Albans, where the family had no connection that I knew of? The questions flooded my head.

Then I took refuge in the fact that no first name for the mother had been mentioned so I decided not to think about it until the birth certificate my cousin Monica had requested arrived. Also, at this time I started to feel a little angry with my cousins for raising the issue at all and that perhaps if it was something my mother wanted to be kept secret then it should remain so. I just wished it would all go away.

In one of Gail's first communications with me, she'd said she was happy and confident in the knowledge that she had found more of her relatives and suggested that for my peace of mind and I should also take the DNA test.

I decided to wait for the birth certificate to come through which a short while later arrived and confirmed the mother's full name as Eileen Hurson (although Mum was Ellen, she always went by Eileen). It also described her as a nurse in a mental hospital which was also correct. Based on this it was pretty clear that my mother had indeed borne a son three years before me. I sent off for my own DNA test and when the result arrived about a month later it showed that Marcus Peck was my nephew and consequently his father Brian was my brother or possibly half-brother.

The thing about DNA is that most of us only know what we see in TV crime dramas when it is used to identify a suspect by comparison with crime scene material. Here the question is straightforward – are these people identical? - and DNA can be categoric about that.

However, it is not so conclusive once relationships become involved because the DNA is diluted with each marriage and subsequent generation, so the conclusions provided by the Ancestry.com analysts are not quite as conclusive as one might wish.

This still left the question of the father's identity unconfirmed. Neither Angela nor I had ever heard from them how long Mum and Dad had known each other before they married; so initially, it seemed possible that the child may have been born of another relationship before they met. However, the more we studied the relevant dates the more unlikely that possibility became.

From my own genealogy research, I had found Dad's army record that showed him joining the army and being posted to a searchlight battery in September 1940 so that gave us the start of a timescale.

The child John Hurson (Brian Peck) was born about nine months later in April or May of 1941, yet my parents were married in May 1942. Was it conceivable that in the space of barely one year my mother had borne a child, recovered enough to rejoin some social life, met Frank Simmons and married him in May 1942 given that he was actually away in the army (although he possibly did have some leave).

Knowing the personalities involved we concluded that the idea was just too outlandish to consider. We had by this time also seen photographs of Brian Peck both as a young man and in later years and whilst he was strongly similar to several of my Hurson uncles there were also clear similarities between him and both my father and me.

On the balance of probabilities, Angela and I feel as sure as we can be that both Mum and Dad were the child's parents and that given the dates involved the pregnancy was most likely the result of a very fond 'farewell' before he went off into the army. So, on the assumption this child was born of a loving relationship, what in heaven's name could have been the reasons for adoption?

To get a sense of what this would have meant to this unmarried couple one has to look back at life as it was then, not through today's eyes. One also has to look at the people involved and their situations and personalities.

My mother Eileen Hurson was a devout Catholic Irish woman in whose veins her faith and the Roman Catholic dogmas she had grown up with ran strongly. For who an unmarried sexual relationship was a mortal sin so the challenge of dealing with the result of this moment's passion, no matter how loving, would have been enormous. Not only would she have been wracked with guilt at her own sinful behaviour but given her knowledge of catholic attitudes to her situation, she would likely have been overwhelmed with fear and anxiety about how the Church and her catholic friends and family would respond.

On a practical level too, she would surely have been at her wit's end. She was pregnant and unmarried with all the general social stigma that carried back then. She had no husband and the closest thing she had to one, Frank Simmons who she might have married had just gone off to war – possibly even to die. She had a job she had to return to as her only means of support. Her situation must have seemed impossible. What to do?

In all of this, there are still two 'unknowns'. One is "Why St Albans?" and the other is "Was Frank Simmons a party to the eventual adoption decision or indeed, did he ever know?"

To deal with the second question first: knowing the character of the two people as we do - they were always a very 'together' couple; Angela and I find it virtually impossible to believe that this was not a joint decision based on the scenario they faced. It seems highly likely that they concluded their situation was so far from ideal, not to say virtually impossible and that, heartbreakingly for them, the child's welfare would be better served if he were adopted.

Concerning whether Frank Simmons knew of the pregnancy, it seems impossible to think otherwise. Being an older conscript, he was never posted abroad until he went briefly to Germany in 1946 on what he always described as 'mopping-up' operations.

Based on searchlight units around the UK from the Orkney Islands to the West Country, all my enquiries suggest that he would have had some home leave during that first year when he could not have been unaware of the pregnancy. He also had leave to get married in May'42 and have a few days honeymoon at Broadstairs in Kent.

As to the St Albans question, frankly, we have no idea but can only speculate. It is so far away from Epsom and Leatherhead in Surrey, Mum and Dad's respective home areas, that it would have been ideal for ensuring that knowledge of her confinement and the birth were kept secret from immediate friends and family. Perhaps a friend or a church connection may have had information about the orphanage in a quiet Hertfordshire village.

ii

So, on now to my sadly never known brother, the late Brian Marcus Peck. Who was this man; this coincidentally named, other Brian?

At the time of writing this, I have not yet met any of my hitherto unknown relatives, although I have corresponded with Marcus Peck and Brian's second wife Thai Peck. Thus far the family seem as interested to know about us and especially my parents (who would also have been Brian's) as Angela and I are to know about them.

Thai has been enormously generous with information about her late husband and it is based on what she has told me that I write the following account of my brother Brian's interesting life. The information is in turn based on what Brian told Thai about his adoption and early life.

As already outlined, my mother Eileen Hurson had a son in 1941 who for reasons we will never be sure of, was placed in an orphanage. His given name at that time was John Hurson which was quite likely after her own father who was a John

One of the carers at the orphanage was a Mrs Peck who over time became very fond of the child John and with her husband decided to adopt him and he became Brian Marcus Peck. After the war, the Pecks divorced and Brian stayed with his mother.

From this point, my grasp of the timeline of Brian's life is a bit tenuous but the dates are not important really and just serve to approximately punctuate the story of the years from then until now.

It seems that following the divorce life was not easy for Mrs Peck and she took a position as housekeeper for a gentleman (a Colonel) of some means who lived in the Horsley area of Surrey. This is something of a coincidence too as in 1975 I was given a posting as the Police Sergeant for Horsley and several nearby villages.

Apparently, the Colonel had a son of a similar age to Brian who attended a well-regarded private school somewhere nearby and he kindly paid for Brian to be placed there too.

In due course, Mrs Peck met Alf Sears who she later married and then emigrated with him to New Zealand where Brian passed the remainder of his childhood. At the end of his formal education, Brian went into journalism gaining his initial experience with the Aukland Star. It was here that he met Kay Townsend whose family had emigrated from Birmingham after the war. Kay was working for a local TV station and it seems they met in a local pub frequented by journalists. They were married in 1963.

Later the same year at the age of twenty-two he moved with Kay to Melbourne, Australia where Aukland Star had given him an introduction to the Melbourne Herald. However, he didn't like it, so when a month or so later the Australia Broadcasting Corporation offered him a job, he jumped at it. (Curiously we could have been pretty close to each other at that time as in the same year when I was eighteen, I visited Melbourne when my P&O ship The Himalaya docked there.)

Brian and Kay had a son Marcus in 1964 and their second child Adam a couple of years later. Sadly, the marriage didn't last and they separated soon after. Following their eventual divorce, Kay met and married Brian Rennie with whom she had two more children and has since become a published author of historical romance novels.

After a time with ABC, Brian became a foreign correspondent and was tasked with covering the continuing war in Vietnam that had been bubbling since the fifties. That infamous conflict saw the US, Australia and other anti-communist allies supporting the south against North Vietnam backed by Russia and China.

As a young reporter still only in his twenties, he found himself reporting from battlefields and cities often under incoming shell or rocket fire. Thai has kindly sent clips of news reports that Brian did on camera from the war zone and it is the strangest feeling to be seeing and hearing this brother I never knew and unbearably sad that I now never will.

Me, the newly promoted police sergeant and Brian Peck the ABC foreign correspondent both aged approx. late twenties.

In September 1968 at Singapore airport, Brian met a pretty young Vietnamese woman on her way back to Saigon. It seems there was an immediate rapport, they stayed in touch throughout his time in Vietnam and a relationship blossomed into love. This young lady was to become his future wife Thai Peck.

However, the route to their future was not smooth as Brian had been previously married and his divorce was not at that time finalised. Also, Thai's parents opposed the match and wanted her to follow their guidance in a choice of husband and marry in the catholic cathedral in Saigon but their daughter had other ideas.

When his tour in Vietnam ended in 1969 Brian returned home to Sydney where in February 1970 Thai joined him and they were married in December 1971.

After some ten years with ABC Brian decided on a change of course and took up a post with the Australian government as an embassy press attaché.

This step required a relocation from Sydney to the state capital Canberra from where he and Thai began ten years of foreign postings the first of which was to Jakarta in Indonesia.

It was in 1975 while they were in Jakarta that the war in Vietnam was coming to its end that would inevitably see Saigon overrun by the communist forces, and thus began a mass exodus of people who had either been openly loyal or politically active in support of the south or who simply didn't fancy staying on there. Among these was Thai's mother, brother and sister for whom she had submitted sponsorship papers to allow them to leave the country and go to Australia.

Her sister's papers went through but her brother was refused permission to leave because he was of military age and her mother would not leave without him so it seemed at first there was no way out until Brian proposed a rescue plan.

He asked for leave from the Embassy to go and help to get them out but this was refused, presumably because it would have been diplomatically indelicate to have a member of embassy staff meddling in Vietnamese affairs, but Brian decided to go anyway.

Armed with all the necessary papers and enough cash to convince corrupt officials to look the other way he headed for Saigon. Apparently, it was not plain sailing nor without personal risk to them all but by use of his local knowledge and connections and a certain amount of subterfuge he managed to get them first to Manila and thence via the US airbase in Guam back to Sydney.

After three and a half years in Jakarta, they were posted to the USA where they stayed for almost six years. Their stay included time in both Washington DC and California.

After around ten years on the diplomatic scene, Brian decided on a change of course and joined a PR company in Melbourne. This was followed by an appointment as Marketing Director with the Australian Business Arts Foundation and then from 2005 as Communications Advisor with Independent Schools Victoria.

Brian sadly died from cancer in April 2015
.

In conclusion and as a tribute to my brother the late Brian Marcus Peck I feel I can do no better than include below a tribute from Michelle Green a former colleague in his last post

Michelle Green   *17 April 2015*

Brian Marcus Peck   8-5-1941 – 10-4-2015

Brian Marcus Peck, 74, died peacefully at home on 10 April 2015, with his loving wife Thai by his side.
Brian's long career in communications began straight after school as a journalist at the Aukland Star in New Zealand. He then worked for 10 years with ABC News, including a stint as a foreign correspondent in war-torn Vietnam. A number of public affairs roles followed that saw him travel the world. He spent 11 years in Jakarta as a Public Affairs Diplomat with the Australian Government, was the Deputy Executive Director, Communications and Marketing Manager for the Australia business arts Foundation, and he also worked with Beyondblue.
When Brian joined Independent Schools Victoria as the Communications Advisor in 2005, I gratefully gained the benefit of his experiences and his accumulated wisdom. The man I knew was a diplomat; he had learned the skills of bringing people together, the power of human connection, the art of giving more than you take.
Brian had a talent for getting to the point without waffle, and in the communications field, there was little that he had not seen or done before. He felt strongly about the power of education and was a fierce advocate for the rights of the child.
That is not to say he was a saint! He did get frustrated at times with jargon, with small-mindedness, with people who focused on small issues at the expense of the bigger picture. Nor was he afraid to use the odd colourful phrase (particularly when supporting his beloved Sydney Swans!).
And yet, since his death, I have received emails from journalists, colleagues and many others, telling me how much Brian has meant to them; the words 'wise, gentlemanly, gentle, enlightened and polite' figure strongly in these messages.
When I asked Thai about Brian, she told me that to understand Brian I needed to know that he was raised with an abundance of love. Lisha, who he always regarded as his true mother, never failed in her love for the blond-haired, blue-eyed boy she could not leave in his orphanage cot.
Brian is survived by his wife, Thai, and four children and their partners: Marcus and Della, Adam and Steph, Sam and Rochelle and Mai Lien and Chris. He is also survived by several grandchildren who adored him.
Thank you, Brian, God bless, and may you cheer on the Sydney Swans to a Grand Final win. In the fullness of time.

…oooOOOooo…

So, after a false conclusion to this memoir at the end of the last chapter that I feel sure left you my reader as surprised as I was, we come now to the real finale.

I am certain that my story has a way to run yet, especially concerning my relationships with this new family. I just hope my now fairly old bones can hang together long enough to enable to me catch up with as many of them that want to meet me. Whether I have time enough left to make the contents of another memoir I seriously doubt as I'm nowhere near as active as in the past which makes having adventures to tell stories about a tad more difficult.

However, being a bit less agile doesn't stop me from holding a camera and venturing out in search of interesting places and people to fill my lens. I will keep posting to my photography website at www.brianseye.co.uk where there is also a blog I use for a bit of public writing or ranting when the fancy takes me.

Once again, thank you for staying the course and at this point, I was going to conclude with the Chinese saying "May you live in interesting times." but I then discovered (fortunately just in time) that it's an ironic expression and actually closer to a curse so let's not go there.

Let me instead close with the Irish departure blessing that I love:

May the road rise up to meet you.

May the wind be always at your back.

May the sun shine warm upon your face;

the rains fall soft upon your fields and until we meet again,

may God hold you in the palm of His hand.

Previous publications by Brian F Simmons

Stepping Out from Ashtead 1944 – 1964

An entertaining look back on twenty years work and play as a boy became a young man in Surrey and far beyond.

ISBN 9781979661539

Until the Lights Went Out
A different sort of police memoir

ISBN 9781983705816

Both books are available as paperback or Kindle via the Amazon site.

With regard to the photography in this book almost all the images are my own but they are far from their best converted to black and white. If you are interested to see more of my wider photographic work, please have a look at www.brianseye.co.uk

Printed in Great Britain
by Amazon